THE BRILL

OF NAKED MIND

SECRET VISIONS

OF

GESAR, KING OF LING

Mountain Treasury Press

1850 Folsom Street #606

Boulder, CO 80302 USA

ISBN-13: 978-0974597416
ISBN-10: 0974597414

THE BRILLIANCE

OF NAKED MIND

SECRET VISIONS

OF

GESAR, KING OF LING

DOUGLAS J. PENICK

CONTENTS

ACKNOWLEDGMENTS

Throughout what follows, the writings, oral instructions and all-pervasive presence of Chogyam Trungpa, Rinpoche, the Sakyong, the Dorje Dradul of Mukpo Dong remain the continuing ground, reference and inspiration.

In many, many places, the profound instruction of His Holiness, Orgyen Kusum Lingpa has left his deep imprint.

The advice and encouragement of the Venerable Tulku Thondup, the late Peter Lieberson, Kidder Smith, Kenneth Green, Joan Anderson, David Warren, Larry Mermelstein, the late Robin Kornman, Karen Hayward, Blake Thompson, Michael Root, Meg Federico, Francesca Fremantle and Helen Berliner have been ever invaluable and unstinting. Important elements of the text would not exist without the tenacity, brilliance, and generosity of Ives Waldo from whose translations many passages are cited and others adapted.

I'd like to thank all of you who are companions on this journey and in this world. This book would not be in your hands without the love, support and hard work of Deborah Marshall.

D.J.P.

Boulder, Colorado

11/05/2011

INTRODUCTION

There is a powerful strand in European thinking that ties knowledge to loss. There is an unbridgeable divide between the physical world, the world of the senses and knowledge. According to this view, understanding, knowledge, wisdom only come into being when the object of that understanding is disappearing or has disappeared.

In this outlook, words come into existence only to signify the absence of their referent. After all, when Itard set out to teach language to the mute wild boy of Aveyron, he taught him the word for milk by taking it away from him. Little wonder then that the child did not learn to speak. He did not wish to be deprived of more. The only other words he learned were "Oh God"!

Theology is a study that arose when God no longer walked with Abraham in the cool of the evening. Petrarch's sonnets arose from the absence of Laura. Dante's divine cosmos radiated from the absence of Beatrice. Folk songs and tales were collected and studied when folk singers and storytellers began to disappear. Anthropology came to exist when the people who were the objects of its study were becoming extinct. The various studies related to ecology now arise as the balance of the natural world appears irretrievably out of kilter.

Our knowledge, both in a scientific and poetic way, seems contingent on loss and absence, and our relationship to the experience of knowing is impoverished and constricted accordingly. We are only prepared for the kind of knowing that emerges when, as Hegel famously put it, "Athena's owl only flies at dusk."

1

In what follows, knowledge, understanding and wisdom pervade the total range of phenomena, arise in the simplicity of the present moment, and expand in continuous and uncontrolled profusion; here wisdom and utter wakefulness have never been separate and remain an endless terrain of ardent exploration. Only a lack of courage and a failure of love can make the world otherwise.

I

DEEDS AND VISIONS
OF GESAR, KING OF LING

*

KING GESAR'S CONQUEST OF THE
DEMON LORD, SATHAM OF JANG

1

Gesar of Ling, the World Renowned Liberator, the Indestructible Conqueror, the Quintessential Hero, the Lord of Warriors and Destroyer of Demons, was sent from the summit of the sky to Tibet, the land of snows, in order to end the domination of the demon kings of the four directions.

After hard won victories over Lutzen, Demon of the North and the Eastern Lords of Hor, he proceeds to do battle with Satham of Jang, Invincible Demon King of the South. Satham is consumed with pride in all he owns and seeks only to expand his realms of pleasure and delight. He enslaves his subjects, dazzling them with promises of extravagant possessions and endless pleasure. He dazzles them with his great beauty, his imperious self-esteem, his luxury and the radiance of his immense golden body which is invulnerable to any attack.

Even the All Victorious Lion Lord's magic crystal sword or lightening-like arrows of meteoric iron cannot pierce the skin of the Demon Lord of Jang. But Gesar devises a lethal ruse. He transforms himself into a flying insect, a small iron bee with razor-edged wings of steel. Then, early one evening as King Satham is indulging in yet another lavish feast amid his generals, followers and family, he raises a toast with a great golden cup of wine. And he slakes his thirst with one huge gulp. Gesar, now a murderous bee, flies into the demon's mouth and down his throat. Then, as he veers hither and yon through Satham's insides, the blades of his wings nick and slice at Satham's lungs, stomach, liver, intestines, kidneys, nerves, arteries and heart. Bit by bit he shreds the demon's insides to ribbons. Surrounded by his helpless courtiers and bodyguards, the Demon King hurls himself on the ground, screaming, rolling back and forth. Writhing and howling like a beast, finally he dies in utter agony.

Satham of Jang's enormous body lies still on the ground like a heap of boulders from a collapsed fortress. His family, friends, soldiers and courtiers stand there frozen; they cannot believe what they are seeing. Then, emerging at the Demon Lord's eyes, ears, mouth, nose, and at the creases of his joints, appearing first as small yellow tongues of flame then as larger orange waves of fire, crackling and snapping, a conflagration emerges and sweeps over the huge corpse. Soon, Satham of Jang has become his own enormous funeral pyre.

From the crown of the demon's head, unseen by anyone, Gesar emerges from the crown of the demon's burning skull.. He has transformed himself into a shimmering ruby-colored fly and flies through the air like an ember. Satham's spirit, now in the form of a shiny onyx-colored fly, follows Gesar and flies off into the smoke.

Then Gesar returns to his accustomed form. Atop his robes of red brocade, he wears gold armor the color of the sun and a crystal helmet that glows like the moon. The white silk banners atop his helmet snap in the wind. He carries his sword, his bow of antelope horn, and in his snow-leopard quiver, his arrows of meteoric iron. For him, no more than a second has passed within the demon's body.

As Satham of Jang's downcast subjects gape, he leaps into the turquoise saddle of his horse of miracles, Kyang Ko Kar Kar. Horse and rider fly up into the blue cloudless sky, where they seem to fuse and became an enormous golden garuda. To a commanding melody, they sing this song:

I, Gesar, the self-born Garuda,

Fly through the pure air of a cool sky,

Open beyond measurement or memory,

And its bright crystal winds pour directly

Through the chambers of my heart.

So, though joyful, the warriors of Ling find the memory of this song haunting as they follow their lord and return home to the Kingdom of Ling.

2

This is the outer story of how Gesar, King of Ling, Indestructible Warrior and Destroyer of Demons defeated the Demon Lord of the South, Satham King of Jang. For a thousand years, men and women have told this story. Some have then written it down, while by others it has been chanted, sung, danced, and acted out. Thus it is famous in every culture throughout the mountains, valleys, plains, and steppes of central Asia.

But there is an inner story of this epic conquest, a secret account, and it is far more strange and unsettling. Here Gesar experienced not just a single great encounter but innumerable encounters. The inner story of Gesar's conquest of Satham of Jang comprises so many tales that Gesar himself could later recall only a relatively small number. Indeed he was or is unsure whether he was or is still experiencing them. However, even if many of Gesar's adventures in the great body of Satham of Jang have become blurred, he has been able to bring back some longer accounts of great spiritual masters and enlightened rulers. How this has come to pass is as follows.

Having assumed the form a small iron bee with furious wings of razor steel, King Gesar waits until the Demon Lord opens his mouth wide. Then, quick as an arrow, he darts into Satham of Jang's cavernous mouth. He streaks past the sharp bronze teeth, and is, sucked in deeper by the demon's gasping breath. Bobbing above the descending purple waves of wine, he hurtles down through the coal black throat. As he presses forward, he slices little holes in the demon's throat. Satham grunts in pain, but thinks it is merely some passing irritation. Then Gesar begins to move though the demon's innards in deadly earnest. He nips and slices at organs, cavities and tendons. Satham now roars in pain. His whole body vibrates like the meeting of two huge cymbals, crushing Gesar until he passes out.

The Great Destroyer of Demons now falls down and down until he crashes to the floor in the depth of the Satham's body.

When he wakes, he finds himself in a vast space filled with dazzling light. Gesar shakes his head and stares in amazement. He has no idea where he is. In front of him is a huge glass tower extending up and up, becoming increasingly brighter at its height. Beyond is a glassy sky of blazing rainbow light, and beneath Gesar's feet is an expanse of dark red glass.

Gesar finds himself lying on a couch of lavender glass; ten chairs of emerald glass and a pink glass table stood nearby. On the table is a black glass tea-pot, a lemon-colored tea bowl and a turquoise glass bell. There are seven red glass windows in the surrounding walls.

Gesar is dazed and puzzled. It takes him some time to realize that all around him the glittering walls are actually made of hundreds of millions of mirrors, mirrors of every size and shape. Ranging up the walls one above the other, they reflect each other's light back and forth, and their light becomes ever more intense. Some of the mirrors nearest Gesar are immense, others are tiny, some are square, others round, still others are as irregular as rain puddles. Some are very old, while others are of a manufacture that can only be imagined as coming from a future. Some are perfect, some are cracked. Some seem to stare at Gesar as if they were alive, while others loom like holes that open onto empty space.

And these are not ordinary mirrors; each bears a label to indicate its special nature. Gesar looks around and sees the Heavenly Emperor Mirror with its gold tiger hook; he sees the White Jade Heart Mirror, the Mirror that is Archer Li, the Blossom Mirror, the Mirror of Torture, the Wind Mirror, and the Self-Doubt Mirror. He sees the Mirror of Man and Woman, the Mirror of Birds, the Mirror of Melody, the Corpse Mirror, the Mirror of Water, The Ice Terrace Mirror, the Mirror of Lust, the Mountain Mirror, the Iron Mask Mirror, the Mirror of Deceit, the Mirror of Me, the Mirror of the Moon, the Mirror in the Shape of the Yong Le Emperor, the Mirror that is Seven Vanished Nations, the Mirror of a Princess pining for a Prince, the Stillness Mirror, the Mirror of Warfare, the Mirror of Nothingness, the Mirror of Bitter Sorrow. He sees the Mirror of the Hangman's Noose, the Mirror of Crushing Fists, the Mirror of Repetition, the Mirror of Saliva, the Mirror with No Words, the Mirror that Holds Back Reflections, the Mirror that is the First Concubine of Emperor Hsuan-yuan, the One Smile Mirror, the Mirror of Rape, the Mirror that is Rice Farmer Chen, the Pillow Mirror, the No-Reflection Mirror, the Flying Mirror, the Horse Mirror, The Mirror of Milk, the Mirror of Perfume. These are only the first mirrors which King Gesar sees within the magical body of King Satham of Jang.

And when he looks into these mirrors, Gesar does not see himself. When merely he glances in one of these mirrors, Gesar enters a completely different world. The world within each mirror has a different sky, different rivers and seas, different plants, suns, moons, stars, animals, cities, men and women. Some are bygone worlds; some are alternate versions of the present and some are unknown futures. Some mirrors show worlds with different physical laws, different customs and different forms of cause and effect. Some worlds are even without light or sun or solidity or space or any movement or thought

9

or emotion. Some are beautiful beyond imagining, others are hells so vile one shrinks to think of them.

And in each of these innumerable new worlds, though Gesar sometimes is someone almost exactly like himself, in others he finds himself to be a new and unimaginable being. He becomes one who is intelligent, stupid, warm, cold, weak, strong, male, female or something in between or both at once or neither at all; sometimes he is human, sometimes a god, hell-being, ghost or beast. He meets gods, warriors, noblewomen, scoundrels, gurus, courtesans, murderers, vagrants, pilgrims, housewives, children, animals, beings of every kind. Sometimes he is an inanimate object and his life, lasting from creation to destruction, is that of a crystal goblet.

In every world, what he must know, must believe, what he must cultivate as wisdom or love, what he must recognize as crime, degradation or virtue, and what he can actually experience as happiness or misery, all are utterly unfamiliar and must be learned anew, if he can learn at all. In some realms, he receives profound, world-altering teachings that he forgets immediately. In others, he has insights that he struggles to retain. But in the torrential succession of experiences, nothing, or almost nothing remains. Gesar glances into each mirror and takes such a new form, he experiences a whole entire life as a new being in a new world from beginning to end; in whatever dramas and struggles that world presents, he lives it out from birth to death.

In uncontrollable frenzy, Gesar flies in and out of mirror after mirror. He is like an insect that must rush from flower to flower to sustain itself. Some worlds seem to last only as long as a caress or the sound of a single note. In other realms, it seems that movement is as slow as the changes in a great mountain range. But he cannot make things go more quickly and he cannot stop to find rest. Worlds begin to blur and blend; only realms that resemble his own original time make the slightest fleeting imprint. His mind becomes nothing but a racing silence or a roaring motionless expanse.

He continues spinning through endless worlds and endless selves. Like a golden bolt of lightning, he flashes from mirror world to mirror world. And each time he enters a world, takes form and dies there, that world dies too; the mirror through which he entered it is shattered. Thus one by one, but at the speed of light, Gesar is destroying every cell in the terrible and wondrous being called Satham of Jang.

So, beginning at the bottom of his torso and rising through his bowels, his stomach his liver and heart and finally to his brain, the Demon King's inner organs desiccate and collapse. At the same time, friction from incessant movement causes the iron bee that is Gesar to become hotter and hotter until he glows like a branding iron. As he passes through King Satham's body, everything he brushes past begins to smolder and catch fire. As he reaches the apex of the demon's skull, the world around him smokes and burns. When finally he escapes through a crack in the Demon King's skull, he hears the faint buzzing of a small black fly following. This insect, the carrion essence of all that once was Satham of Jang disappears in the smoke.

For a few moments or possibly much longer, Gesar is not sure what world he has now entered. He is not certain that he has returned to his true home world. The sky seems not quite so high or bright, the grass seems a different shade of green. When he sees the Miracle Horse, Kyang Ko Kar Kar waiting for him, his steed seems slightly different; the way he shifts his weight is not quite the same. And when Gesar resumes his accustomed guise, his armor seems heavier, his helmet tighter; his weapons have a slightly different balance. He wonders if indeed he has entered a slightly different realm. And he realizes that there is no way that he will ever know.

Gesar, Lion King of Ling, Destroyer of the Demons, The Peerless Warrior has no choice. He leaps into the turquoise saddle of his horse of miracles, Kyang Ko Kar Kar. The two fly up into the pale blue cloudless sky, where they seem to fuse. They become an enormous golden garuda, floating on immense vulture-like wings in the center of the sky. Then Gesar sings this song:

Not relying on anything,

 Not prolonging anything,

Not hastening anything to its end:

Here the dramas of life swell and resolve without a trace

As a rainbow pulsing in the sky.

The great heart-beat of experience shimmers

As the tints of color in this arc of light.

On such magical sky bridges do men and women,

Demons, and gods wander and play out

Their poignant deeds of hope and fear.

I, Gesar, the self-born Garuda,

Fly through the pure air of an endless sky,

Open beyond measurement or memory,

And its bright crystal winds pour directly

Through the chambers of my heart.

The warriors of Ling are haunted by this song as they follow their lord and return home to the Kingdom of Ling.

3

When Gesar has returned to Ling, he sits on his throne and wears the golden robe that commemorates his triumph over Satham of Jang. Now he feels millions upon millions of other worlds nearby and myriad other Gesar beings very much alive. He feels that in every instant, with each blink of an eye or turn of his head, he shifts slightly from one world to another. When he sleeps, he feels he is living out other fates in other realms. Every world he passes through calls forth waves of his love and his devotion, but there is no certainty or substance. His victories over demonic obsession, for all their courage, pain and sacrifice, will never bring a sure conclusion.

Gesar does not know if the heroes he believes in exist or ever existed in this world, whether their stories are or ever were true here, or whether they will later find a world where they may yet be true. He does not know if he heard accounts of renowned mahasiddhas in his dreams. He does not know why he would find descriptions of the rulers of Shambhala familiar. Nonetheless, he writes them down as he might write a wistful love poem to a woman he knew by name only.

What follows now are an invocation to Tilopa, the life stories of Kukkuripa, Kankala and Mehkala, King Indrabhuti, and an account of the rulers of Shambhala.

Gesar finds himself in the Buddha's birthplace, Lumbini Grove. He sees the Buddha's mother, leaning against a tree, about to give birth. He sees everything in this universe reflected in the abdomen of Queen Maya. As is said:

"Then from every one of her hair-pores, in all these worlds, emerge visions of all the past lives and future lives of the Awakened One, as he appeared and will appear in every universe, world, land, and place; all appear just as sun, moon, stars, planets and clouds are reflected in a lake, a piece of gold, a mirror, or in a crystal bowl of water.

"Even as these self-expanding waves of life penetrate Gesar, King of Ling, a charnel ground yogi gives him this invocation and feast offering."

*

THE STREAM OF SELF-EXISTING FIRE:

A GURU YOGA FEAST INVOKING

THE LIFE FORCE OF LINEAGE,

THE DEATHLESS TILOPA

Gathered here in the charnel ground of all phenomena

Surrounded by the corpses of rotting hopes, false assumptions,

Decaying love, possessions that will soon be stolen away;

Sitting amidst the ashes of dreams and secret ambitions,

The air is choked with the smoke of ignorance

That renders all around us almost invisible;

Here we are paralyzed by the winds of hope and fear

As predatory ghosts of uncertainty, doubt, and anguish swirl about.

Confessing our myriad delusions,

O Tilopa,

We look for you, the fount of lineage,

The father of refuge.

Aspiring to see the living face of enlightenment

In the darkness of this world,

We call on you.

2

Now, on this powerless ground of utter futility,

Arise from the eternal womb of emptiness,

Telo come here in this very place

Come here and display the Vajra Dance

Utterly consume this Vajra Feast.

In consuming the offering of food,

Display the living body of reality.

In accepting the offering of song,

Display the living speech of reality.

In consuming the offering of amrita,

Display the living mind of reality.

I offer myself in body speech and mind.

Please take your seat here.

Please show yourself now as life itself .

3

Accepting these offerings,

Consuming us utterly,

Though you do not move or stir,

We request you now to appear.

As you crush the husk of a body that clings to an I,

May we meet you face to face

In the living paths of development and completion.

As you crush the husk of a body that clings to an I,

May we meet you face to face

In the living experience free from bias.

As you crush the husk of samsara itself,

May we meet you face to face

In the living bond of samaya.

As you crush the husk of a body that arises from karma,

May we meet you face to face

Consumed in the commitment of inner heat.

As you crush the husk of a body that clings to an I,

May we meet you face to face

In the limitless illusion of embodiment.

As you crush the husk of the three worlds,

May we meet you face to face

In the luminous expanse of dream.

As you crush the husk of a body that clings to an I,

May we meet you face to face

In the unimpeded flow of all-pervasive luminosity.

As you crush the husk of a body that tends to clings to an I,

May we meet you face to face

In passing freely from illusory life to life.

As you crush the husk of a body that cling to an I,

May we meet you face to face

In completely transforming the apparition of existence.

As you crush the husk of craving in the duality of samsara and
nirvana,

May we meet you face to face

In the one taste of great bliss.

Offering the mudra to the Guru who is Buddha himself,

May we meet you face to face

In the great mirror of Mahamudra which is Reality itself.

Offering you our body as the mandala of existence,

May we live in the ever present spontaneous union

Of mother and child luminosity

Inseparable from your body, speech, and mind

In the ceaseless co-emergence of the bardo.

4

Here, by the power of life itself,

You arise unborn

From the red thousand-petalled lotus

Which is the spontaneous flowering,

The living purity of all outer and inner phenomena,

The secret space of Prajnaparamita.

Seated with your left leg down and your right knee raised,

Your naked body shimmers

Like the pale autumn sky at sunrise.

You are covered with ash.

Your wild black hair is bound up into a loose top-knot.

Your blood-shot eyes burn like the noon sun.

Your face is sun-burned and unshaven.

You grimace and your sharp irregular teeth clash

With the sound of breaking glass.

You smile lasciviously

And every movement of the air seems melodious.

Your expression, is shameless, impenitent,

Lustful and indifferent.

In your right hand, you hold a living silver fish

Whose red guts hang from its belly.

In your left hand you hold an ancient skull-cup

Brimming with liquor.

Your scent is tangy and feral.

You are still as a wolf awaiting its prey.

You are luminous as the full moon at midnight.

Suddenly, you arise on your seat

In the shimmer of all perception.

Suddenly you sing

In the beating heart of the body.

You are presence itself.

5

In endless union with the self-existing consort,

In the yoga of Chandali,

You are the heat of fire.

In endless union with the self existing consort,

In the yoga of illusory body,

You are the solidness of earth.

In endless union with the self existing consort,

In the yoga of dream,

You are the movement of wind.

In endless union with the self existing consort,

In the yoga of luminosity,

You are primordial space.

In endless union with the self existing consort,

In the yoga of transference,

You are the pervasiveness of water.

In endless union with the self existing consort,

In the yoga of bardo,

You are consciousness itself.

In inseparable non-dual union,

You dwell in the empty essence

In the luminous heart of the primordial consort

Where all inner and outer phenomena

Rise, dwell and die.

Free from experience,

You are not born;

You do not remain;

You do not die.

OM AH HUM

TILO, TILO TILO

HRIH AH HAM

AH AH AH HUM PHAT

6

Sought in the mirage of appearance,

You change form and disappear.

Found in the mirage of appearance,

You are mute.

Supplicated in the mandala of appearance,

You show the luminous empty heart

Piercing through all the illusions of pleasure and pain.

All that exists and does not exist,

All that moves and does not move,

All that is mind and is beyond mind,

Offering and offered inseparable,

Swirls in your kapala.

RAM YAM KAM

Unborn,

As our senses shine.

This is the direct experience

Of Tilopa, the corpse,

The natural kingdom of body.

Living,

As the seasons pass.

This is the direct experience

Of Tilopa, the root,

The unceasing power of speech.

Without past

As in the alternation of day and night,

This is the direct experience

Of Tilopa, the tree,

The deathless lineage co-emergent wisdom.

Beyond awareness

There is reality here and now.

This is the direct experience

Of Tilopa, the stream,

Ungraspable, complete, alive.

Experience now

The bliss of Tilopa's mind:

This unborn word:

This naked world.

7

These are the oral instruction which Tilopa himself sang to Naropa.

You are a worthy vessel.

In the monastery of Pullahari,

In the limitless expanse of luminosity, beyond concept,

The sparrow of mind, moving from life to life,

Has flown on the wings of co-emergence.

Do not yearn for belief in a self.

In the monastery of non-dual prajna,

In the offering pit of the illusory body,

By the radiance of awareness rising from the bliss and heat of inner heat,

The fuel of the kleshas and conventional concepts

Of body, speech and mind has been burnt up.

Do not pine for the duality of this and that.

In the monastery free from words and concepts,

The sharp knife of prajna,

Of Mahasukha, of Mahamudra

Has cut the rope of ambition in the bardo.

Dismiss the craving which causes all attachment.

Walk the hidden path of the Wish-Fulfilling Gem

Leading to the realm of the heavenly tree, the changeless.

Untie the tongues of mutes.

Stop the stream of samsara, of belief in a self.

Recognize your true nature as a mother knows her child.

Prajna is self-aware,

Beyond the path of speech

And the object of no thought whatsoever .

I, Tilopa have nothing at which to point.

Know this as pointing in itself to itself.

Do not imagine, think, deliberate,

Meditate, act, but be at rest.

Do not be concerned with any object.

Reality, self-existent, radiant,

In which no memory can disturb you,

Cannot be called a thing.   (1)

8

O great Tilopa

O incomparable

O unborn and deathless one,

As you have never departed,

By your unsparing kindness,

May we remain in the Great Inseparability

Of your unchanging body speech and mind.

If there is any continuity of anything,

It is you.

If there is any lineage of anything anywhere,

It is you.

If there is love,

It is you.

By the power of your motiveless intention

Which fills the sky like ceaseless wind,

May every illusory being,

Drifting frantically through the skies like dust

Find completion

In the uncontrived and luminous mandala of your being.

AH AH AH

*

And again that same yogi whispered to King Gesar:

Unborn,

The senses shine.

This is the direct experience

Of Telopa, the corpse,

The natural kingdom of body.

Living,

The seasons emerge.

This is the direct experience

Of Telopa, the root,

The unceasing power of speech.

Without past

In the alternation of day and night,

This is the direct experience

Of Telopa, the tree,

The deathless lineage co-emergent wisdom.

Beyond awareness

There is reality.

This is the direct experience

Of Telopa, the stream,

Ungraspable, complete, alive.

Experience now

The bliss of Telopa's mind:

This unborn word:

This naked world.

THE LIFE OF KUKKURIPA

At another moment, near the bodhi tree in Bodhgaya, Gesar sees the great sage Megashri. The sage sings wordlessly and displays to Gesar incalculable, uncountable, immeasurable, inconceivable incomprehensible, inestimable numbers of Buddhas. He shows Gesar as many Buddhas a there are atoms in all the continents and as many Pure Land of there are stars in all the galaxies. Gesar sees Buddhas in innumerable fixed and changing forms, all radiating light in networks of rays of many colors, pervading all conceivable world systems, uniting them in a vast total pattern which is beyond conception or comprehension or truth or falsehood. The great sage shows Gesar the infinity of intersecting nets that are the inseparable nature of light and awareness. The great sage conveys to Gesar, King of Ling, the Peerless Warrior the words that follow.

*

THE BLAZING MIRROR

OF ABSOLUTE COMPASSION:

INVOKING THE SUPREME MAHASIDDHA

KUKKURIPA,

THE CO-EMERGENT KING OF ILLUSION

1.i

In the taste of sukra,

Thought spontaneously returns to non-thought.

Known directly in the gate of passion

Which no concept can penetrate,

Inseparable light and life force,

Pulse with primordial Great Bliss.

The stainless expanse of boundless compassion,

Radiant with the four joys,

Ceaselessly emanates and gathers without motive or direction.

Beyond all worlds, it offers and receives the world.

Homage to this, the self-born mind of Kukkuripa

Who, hearing the cries of illusory worlds

Moves through the empty realms of form.

Everywhere.

1.ii

Though called Kukkuripa

Born from the unchanging bindu,

His family name cannot be known.

Though known as Shantibhadra,

His birth name cannot be remembered.

He appeared suddenly in the eastern part of Bengal.

He appeared later as monk and pandita at glorious Nalanda

Where he mastered the twelve branches of scripture of the two vehicles.

But hearing the echo of Maitreya's whisper on an evening breeze,

He moved to seek the luminous great expanse

Pulsing in the symbolic forms free from habitual tendencies.

He moved to a forest cave near Lumbini

To practice in uninterrupted solitude.

1.iii

For twelve years, one pointedly,

Free from acceptance and rejection,

Kukkuripa practiced in this way:

The radiance which arises at the moment of death

Is the luminosity of Dharmakaya.

Seeing everything in sensory reality as unelaborated Dharmakaya

Brings this inner radiance to the path.

To purify all habitual tendencies of the illusory body,

And bring them to the path,

The essence of all meditation is the Great Compassion.

By meditating on the seed syllables, Buddhas and Buddha fields

The circumstances of being born into a particular place and body

Are completely purified.

Thus all the physical world is the pure body of enlightenment;

Hearing all sound is the pure speech of enlightenment;

Experiencing all the movements of mind is the pure mind of
enlightenment.

So by one pointed meditation

On the stainless empty nature of phenomena

And Lokeshvara's all-pervasive love,

Kukkuripa was firmly established in utpattikrama

And achieved the worldly siddhis:

Swift movement, penetration of matter, clairvoyance,

Flying, invisibility, immortality, complete health, and the rest.

In this way, he lived alone deep within the forest,

Eating fruit and nuts, and wild yams,

Drinking water from a nearby stream.

One day a small black dog,

A female puppy, starving and lice-ridden,

Ventured into his cave.

For three days, lovingly he fed and nursed the dog.

1.iv

But then Kukkuripa heard the voice of Indra

And rose up far above the cloudy summit of Mt. Meru,

To the Place of Auspicious Vision,

The realm of the thirty-three gods of the desire realm,

And the secret dwelling of the Yaksas.

In the shining center of this realm,

Encircled by a hundred jeweled turrets

And encompassed by a golden wall,

Stands Indra's court, the Victorious Abode.

Sixteen thousand jewel columns form the terraces of the palace

And support its golden roofs.

Five hundred gods guard its four gates in each of the four directions.

Below the ground is soft as silk but made of gold

And sprinkled with jewels of a hundred and one hues.

In each direction stands a park outside the city walls,

And fragrant gardens border each of these parks.

Everywhere are magical elephants, horses, thousands of attendants.

Yaksa vajra-holders dwell in the four mounds

At the four corners of Mt. Meru's summit.

Beyond the parks to the northeast stands the All Gathering Tree,

The source of fulfillment of all wishes.

Beneath it lies a square white stone slab, glowing like moon light.

In the southeast is the great crystal vase of amrita,

Protecting the gods from sickness, aging and sudden death.

The air is filled with the endless reverberation of a drumbeat

Echoing the truths of impermanence, suffering, emptiness,

Pulsing with the thought of nirvana as eternal peace.

Southwest of the court is the circular gathering place

Where the gods hear the excellent law.

In its center is a great golden throne.

Here Indra sits as he teaches the gods seated around him.

Around glorious Indra, radiant as the noon-day sun,

Sit the thirty-two: eight are the gods of wealth,

Then the Asvin twins, lords of fertility and harvest,

The eleven wrathful protectors, and the twelve lesser suns.

All these deities appear in this realm in their own form

And, simultaneously, as the places and qualities of that realm.

This is the expanse of the phenomena created by desire.

1.v

Measureless in its array of subtle harmonies and insights,

Utterly absorbing all restless dissatisfactions of mind,

In this glittering realm of infinite delicacy,

Only a hair's breadth of difference separates outer and inner worlds.

So overwhelmed by waves of pleasure and gratitude

Kukkuripa lingered there for what seemed many years.

Yet one day, he thought of the small dog, left starving in his cave.

He called out to the gods:

"Let us all descend now to the land of Jambudvipa."

And when they asked why, he told them of the dog

Which must even now be dying without water and food.

"Ah, " they replied, "Even though you have practiced for so long,

You are still attached to the idea of a dog."

And persuaded by this argument, Kukkuripa remained for 12 more years.

But the thought of the dog's suffering of thirst and starvation,

Its pains and terror in dying,

The rotting of its body, its bones turned to dust

Would not be dispelled.

Then, in the company of all the gods,

Kukkuripa sang this song:

"Because emptiness is experienced as void;

Because life is experienced as the limit of a self;

Because light is experienced as knowing;

Because compassion is experienced as an action;

Because perceptions are experienced as attributes;

Because bliss is experienced as pleasure;

You great gods and your domain are conditional and illusory,

And you must cling to limits imposed by desire, sensation and mind.

"But know, my friends, that the infinite delights here

Are equaled by the intensity of terror and regret

That you will find when your beautiful bodies suddenly begin to age

And your sublime domain dissolves

In the smoke of the charnel ground and smell of rotting flesh.

"While you still can, realize that you and your realm

Have risen as a spontaneous gift of primordial Great Compassion

From the radiance of Buddha Amitayus, Lord of Boundless Life,

As a shadow of his deathless pure realm

Seen dimly through the screen of your desires.

"Now by opening your hearts and thoughts to the flow

Of Great Compassion, which is the free breath of endless life,

The senses themselves become the self-existing gateways

To unconditioned life, all-pervasive light, and compassion
Free from the chains of desire and fear."

Fear froze the minds of all the gods,
And with longing they listened.

Kukkuripa then showed the Buddha's way
Of entering the Pure Realm Of Amitayus,
Self-Born Lord of Boundless Life
To all the gods, Yaksas and other deities.

2.i

Pointing to the sun, to water, to earth, and so forth,
He showed them in this way:

"Gazing at the sun, brilliant, nurturing, and all-pervasive
As it hangs in the Eastern sky like a suspended drum,
Let the continuity of radiant light remain clear and unchanging
Whether one's eyes are open or closed.

"Gazing on pure water, let it fill your mind.
As it becomes ice, shining and transparent.

40

It becomes a deep blue ground of lapis lazuli,

Shining from within and without,

Lit by the vast sparkling jeweled cloth of gold beneath it.

This water, radiant, insubstantial and ever moving

Is the ground of all qualities and aspirations.

"From the substantial and enduring qualities of earth,

An immeasurable expanse of jeweled palaces arise,

Adorned with garlands of pearls, diamonds, rubies, and liquid gold,

Surrounded by rows of trees with jewel leaves

From whose branches hang sweet ripe fruit.

From this earth comes the solid form of all qualities and aspiration.

"From the ever moving quality of air

Arise vivacious perfumes and subtle promptings.

All sounds become melodious .

From this air comes the movement of aspiration.

"Free from illusory longings or fixed desires,

The elements, from their own nature,

Are joined in perfect permanent accord.

This glimpse of Amitayus' Pure Realm

Purifies eons of evil deeds and habitual perceptions.

"Here in the light of the jeweled leaves of each tree,

An infinite number of Buddhas like fine dew

Radiate light into an infinity of pure and impure realms.

All the waters, palaces, and so forth

Also sparkle with the blazing of countless hosts of Buddhas

Filling the whole of space.

"In the center, like the sun at the center of all light rays in the world,

The Buddha Amitayus, radiant like molten gold,

Sits on his blazing lotus throne.

The Tathagata's body is the body of the Dharmadhatu,

And inseparable from the 8 consciousnesses,

The qualities of your own mind, innate and radiant.

"At that moment, all the Buddhas and Bodhisattvas

Send out streams of golden light bathing all of phenomena.

Then one hears the path of liberation spontaneously

Echoing in streams of water, breezes, the stirring of leaves,

Bird songs and flickers of light.

"You are completely inseparable

From Buddha Amitayus, boundless life itself;

From Buddha Amitabha, who is infinite light;

And from Avalokiteshvara, the embodiment of compassion

Unlimited by ordinary concepts of space, time, or difference.

"Now, or later when the karma which has bound the elements

In this realm and being dissolves,

Rely on this.

"As subtle movements of air in air,

All dualistic struggles are dissolved in boundless life.

As sunlight colored in shifting clouds,

All delusory passions are dissolved in boundless light.

As mind taking shape in myriad illusory phenomena,

All suffering and fear of suffering are dissolved in limitless compassion.

You are no longer restricted by the limits of being, time, or realm.

"So, be it in one place or many; be it all at one time or in many times.

Wherever there is imprisonment in pain and confusion,

You will appear there to liberate beings from suffering.

"Be it in one place or many, be it all at one time or in many times,

Wherever the Tathagata appears,

You will appear to hear and praise that one.

"Because the Tathagata is the heart of all life,

These two activities are identical."

Thus dissolving all absorption in the realm of the thirty-three gods,

Kukkuripa re-entered the human realm.

3.i

When the Acarya had returned to his forest cave,

The dog he had left behind ran up to him.

She had neither starved nor aged.

It seemed as if he had been gone for no more than a day,

And might have seemed no more than an instant,

Except that in his absence,

The puppy had dug out a pit in the rear of the cave,

And there a spring of crystal water rose.

Seeing it, Kukkuripa heard in the bubbling water's play

The clear voice of Nagarjuna himself:

"Water lying deep within the earth

Rises immaculate and pure,

Like pure wisdom which seemed lost and locked

In the obscurations of this world."

Then Kukkuripa picked up the black she-dog,

Held it in his lap and caressed it,

And he did so, the dog became the yogini

Radiant in the full bloom of youth,

Splendid with all the major and minor marks.

3.ii

Then Vajrayogini, in a voice

With the sound of an approaching summer thunder-storm,

Called to the Acarya:

"In the deathless pulse of limitless compassion,

Radiant, all-penetrating, unfixed,

45

There is no obstacle or antidote.

The relative and absolute,

The momentary and the timeless do not separate.

"In the unfabricated samadhi, there is no attainment.

So it is said:

'Supremely unchanging great passion is primordial awareness.'

"Light and life force joined

In the gate of passion

As temporary conventional bliss

Is inseparable from bliss beyond concept.

"Expanding and gathering

This bliss is the direct expression of limitless compassion."

3.iii

Then in a haunting and melodious soft voice,

Like the sound of a bird leaving the nest,

The Yogini sang to him:

"You have emptied the god realm, O son of Noble Family.

You have done well to return here.

"The pure and free expanse of sunyata

Is not reached by the contrived path of rejecting the world.

The changeless radiance of Great Compassion

Is not reached by the fabricated path of clinging to good
qualities.

"Here, now this very place is

The living reality of compassion.

"Here the six realms and the trikaya

Are simultaneous.

This can only be seen in the light

Of all-inclusive Great Compassion,

Which is the Great Bliss.

"This world, exactly as it is,

The body, speech and mind of all the Buddhas,

Here, now and always reaches out to you.

"Now, in this very instant, here on this very spot,

The Dakini opens the unfabricated treasury of the innate,

The stainless great bliss, ever undispersed.

"Thus, from the universal heart of ceaseless compassion itself

Known only by direct experience

In the treasure-house of phenomenal existence,

The Four Abhishekas spontaneously arise.

3.iv

Kukkuripa and the Yogini were henceforth inseparable.

This is the uncontrived samaya,

The primordial ground,

The unmistaken path,

The fruition which needs no confirmation

Even by experience itself.

This is the unimpeded living expression

Of space in union with space.

Free from intention or effort,

Samatha, natural motionless non-thought;

Vipassana, natural movement devoid of attachment;

Inseparable: this is the authentic Mahavipassana

Of ceaseless Great Compassion.

Should even the notion of an obscuration arise,

Should even subtle duality appear momentarily real,

Let it melt in that motiveless embrace

Which is Buddha-nature itself.

Receive the unfathomable offerings

Of shimmering senses and torrential passions

Arising from the primordial union of bliss and emptiness

As the spontaneous ganachakra

Consumed by joy,

Consuming it.

Consumed by desolation.

Consuming it.

Consumed by mystery,

Consuming it.

Consumed by terror,

Consuming it.

Consumed by sickness,

Consuming it.

Consumed by gratitude,

Consuming it.

Giving and consuming all.

Nothing is excluded.

There is no remainder,

As the wisdom flames

Dance madly in the empty sky.

3.v

Kukkuripa then sang this song:

"Married to one whose mind is the sky,

My abandonment within phenomena cannot be described.

"Abandoned, I see the source and origin.

O Mother, the child I see here cannot, in truth, be seen.

"From my first childbirth came a son,

His being made from sensations, memory, emotional tendencies.

Cutting the umbilical cord,

He too is abandoned.

"Cut down to the root,

My birth and youth are fulfilled."

Kukkuripa says: "This is firm.

Whoever understands this is a hero."

3.vi

Moving as the directionless wind of great compassion

Through the infinite open expanse of pure illusion,

Appearing in a galaxy forms,

Appearing in an infinite expanse of realms and places,

Appearing in words and outside of words,

The Mahasiddha Kukkuripa

Is said to have dwelt in Lumbini and Kapilavastu.

He is said to have brought back many tantras from the Dakini realm.

He is said to have liberated innumerable beings.

Padmavajra who taught Telo who taught Naro

Is said to be his student.

Sent by Naropa, Marpa of Lhodrak met him

And received the Mahamaya and its three yogas from him.

At that time, Mahasiddha Kukkuripa lived in the south

On a mountain island in the center of a boiling poison lake.

He appeared there as a dark human form, the color of a rotten corpse.

His body was covered with hair and his face was like a monkey's.

Marpa found him lying still beneath a tamarind tree,

Covered with bird feathers, his face hidden in the crook of his arm.

A black female dog slept next to him.

Now, this great lord dwells in the sky of the Dakini realm,

Where he is the unwaning moon and ever-rising sun.

His indestructible three gates

Are passport and entry into all pure realms.

Awake, completely free, alive, sudden and direct

He is Buddha Amitayus, Boundless Life.

His signless mind is living reality itself.

Blazing with passion, stirring every movement of the mind,

He is Buddha Amitabha, Boundless Light.

His voice is the brilliance of love and source of all clarity.

Reaching out in all phenomena considered as other,

He is Avalokiteshvara, ever responding to all suffering.

His body is the ever-present world of the senses.

Free in all the illusory dimensions of space and time,

Savoring everything,

He is self-born Great Compassion, running wild.

MAHA KARUNA MAHA SUKHA SUDDHA SARVA SVAHA

1.4 THE LIFE OF KANKALA AND MEHKALA

Gesar, King of Ling sees himself wandering at Sarnath in the gathering darkness of late evening. A young girl appears from the dark and gives him a text. He cannot read it because then the Queen of Night encompasses him.

Emerging from every shining pore of the Queen of Night's velvet body, Gesar sees all the sentient beings, gods, demigods, humans, animals, ghosts, hell-beings with all their varying capabilities and interests in all their disparate abodes. Some are joyful, others suffer unspeakably. Amongst them, he sees innumerable beings trying to dispel the ignorance and relieve the suffering of those around them. They are like the immeasurable flickers of light rising and falling on a vast torrential night sea.

*

THE RAZOR OF PRAJNA:

CALLING ON THE ALL-PERVASIVE

SARVABUDDHADAKINI,

THE FEARLESS AND RADIANT ONES,

MAHAYOGINIS MEKHALA AND KANAKHALA

1.i

Appearing in her unassimilable display,

Appearing without thought in form after form,

She dances the endless winds of mind-made karma

That pour through the empty chambers of the heart,

Tearing apart the heart of form and giving birth.

Homage to her who is the offering,

The offerer, and the object of the offering;

The sacrifice, the sacrificer, the object of the sacrifice.

One in the vast emptiness of the guru's mind.

1.ii

Mekhala and Kanakhala were sisters born to a householder in Maharastra. Mekhala was two years older than Kanakhala. Their father felt fortunate to betroth them in their childhood to the two sons of a wealthy merchant, and years later was beside himself with pleasure when the marriages finally took place.

Though both the merchant's sons were, to all appearances, entirely respectable, in fact the elder one was perversely dissolute while the younger one was cold and cared only for business. Mekhala, for her husband's amusement, was forced to subject herself to the sexual usage of his friends; while Kankhala was neglected and continually criticized by her husband's family for failing to please him. Mekhala found herself being secretly debased into something with less self-respect than a slave. While Kanakhala found herself becoming a wraithlike demoness, consumed by resentment and bitterness.

When they sat together, recalling their childhood, so filled with delight, excitement, and curiosity, they could not understand why they were now so tortured and their life so painful and unrecognizable. Their sorrow was all the greater since their own family would not listen and would not permit them to return home.

"Is there a bridge that can cross over this wasteland of evils and suffering? Is there any way we can change our lot in this world?" they often wondered as they sat together on a balcony which overlooked the busy street on which their husbands' shop was situated.

And often they talked of running away to another country. But, as two lone women, they knew they would be treated just as badly wherever they went. They could see no possible escape.

As they were conversing in this way one evening, it happened that the great guru, Kanha was passing by in the street below. Kanha was unshaven and very dark. His eyes were bloodshot, his gaze steady and imperious. As he walked proudly through the street surrounded by seven hundred male and female disciples, seven yellow silk canopies floated in the air above his head, and seven hand drums hovered and played in the air around him.

The sisters were filled with awe. They decided at once that they should seek out Kanha and ask him for the way to alleviate their suffering. When Kanha received them, they said:

"We live in terror of this world of continuous and inescapable pain. Please show us the path which can liberate us from the iron net in which we are enmeshed by causes we do not know."

Thus they begged the great guru. Seeing the intensity of their revulsion and longing, he empowered them with the sadhana of Vajravarahi and the instructions on the complete integration of inseparable view, meditation, action and result. He sent them off to practice in solitude in the forest, and they did so for twelve years. Though their husbands, family and friends searched everywhere they could think of, they could not find them. All those who had known them were sure that they had died.

1.iii

Through one pointed devotion and practice, the sisters received the blessings of Vajravarahi. Both sisters attained the powers of pacifying, enriching, magnetizing and destroying. They mastered the outward gazes whereby the world is transformed along with all other mundane siddhis. They were no longer impeded by mountains, walls or water, nor did they experience the sorrow of any inner impediments. Without deviating for an instant from their vows, they practiced continuously.

One day as they were walking near their hermitage, they encountered followers of the Mahasiddha Goraksa who challenged them: "If you are students of the great Kanha, then show us some miracle."

It happened that these yogins all lived in an especially lovely place. So the girls, unwilling to hear their guru disparaged, performed the gaze called, "that which moves forth". They looked in the direction of these yogins' retreat and moved their dwellings to a white ashy desert which was neither beautiful nor pleasant. The sisters then said to the yogins: "Now you must honor your guru by restoring your retreat place." This they could not do. Later, only when Goraksa himself asked the sisters to forgive his disciples, they restored the houses to their former locale.

1.iv

After some time, both sisters felt a longing to see Kanha once again, and went off in search of him. They found him in Hemadala in Eastern Bengal where he had gone to bring the King, Lalitacandra to the path of dharma. The great teacher sat amid thousands of his disciples, and spent his days teaching and performing feast offerings in the eight charnel grounds which surrounded that city.

Pressing through the throng surrounding Kanha, the sisters called out to him, prostrated, and made mandala offerings. The great guru smiled and spoke kindly but did not recognize them. The sisters were no longer the young wives of wealthy men but now resembled wild dark forest creatures. He asked them who they were.

Mekhala and Kanakhala were shocked that their guru did not know them. After all they had spent years and years practicing and living according to his instructions. They did not know what to think. Their minds went blank, and they were struck dumb. In that same moment, they recognized that the powers they had attained in practice were merely worldly attainments. Such achievements were relative and impermanent. Then as if looking at a cosmic snare, they saw the unending intricacy of cause and effect that is mind itself. Their beings were flooded by light without origin.

Mekhala sang this song:

"Beyond attachment, all inner and outer phenomena

Are mind and have one taste.

In the supreme meditation without effort or striving,

Perfect Buddhahood radiates pure non-dual bliss."

Kanakhala sang this:

"Wearing impenetrable armor of patience,

Crowned with vajra endurance,

In my own mind, I set forth.

Now I leap from the human corpse."

The Mahacarya replied: "That being so, certainly you should have brought me an offering"

And the sisters told him: " Now, by the grace of the guru, we two have attained our goal, we wish only to dissolve into the sky. We will be pleased to offer whatever the guru requests."

The Mahacarya replied: " Well then, cut off your heads, and give them to me"

II

So, without intention or self-conscious drama, the meeting of guru and disciple proceeded in the unfolding of Buddha-mind itself. From their mouths, the sisters each drew out the diamond sword of prajna.

Mekhala and Kanakhala, held the blazing swords which had sprung from their mouths like tongues of flame aloft in their right hands and swirled them in the air. The sound was harsh and terrifying like the roar of an approaching tornado.

Then the sisters sang:

"Listen,

The melody of the sword of prajna

Calls forth time in

The appearance of reality;

So filled with subtle meanings, questions, promptings,

Worlds radiate in the unceasing movement of sound.

Opening and closing

The shape of the world and the experience of beings

Expands and contracts.

Life begins, remains, echoes, and decays.

Sound in its coloration,

As blue, yellow, scarlet, green;

Shimmers as the mandala of existence,

Solidifies in waves of words as ground of being:

As anger, pride, lust, and envy, fear;

As the demarcation of what is called life

And what is called death

Spins unceasingly, pressing on

As the dim welter of conflicting emotion.

It is said:

'Just as a moment has an end,

So it must have a beginning and a middle.'

So, from the naming of one moment,

The infinite mirage of time appears:

The mirage of beginning, of maintaining, of destruction and of
void.

At a word or phrase

The senses expand, contract:

As space and solidity

Where beings seek to dwell.

Worlds take form.

Those who live there live in time,

Struggle to give birth, to continue, to die.

So illusory dramas of life and death are strategized and played

As beings seek refuge in endless realms,

Bound together inextricably

By concept and word."

2.ii

Then as suddenly as a flash of lightning cuts through a mass of black
thunder-clouds, the sisters slashed through their necks completely. And
although they severed head from body, their heads remained poised
upon their necks.

"In utter simplicity

As the stainless and unfabricated sword of prajna

Moves like a great wind

Through the all unstable certitudes of thought and emotionality

Which beings try to make their home,

All complex logics

Collapse.

All struggles

Dissolve.

Cut through all intentions of beginning, or speculation about origins,

Of needing to initiate anything or for anything to be or have been initiated.

Cut anxiousness.

Cut causality away.

Cut through all ideas of and strategies for preserving, maintaining, or continuing,

Of needing to preserve anything or for it to be preserved.

Cut emotionality.

Cut hope away.

Cut through all thoughts of loss, of death, or annihilation,

Of needing to extinguish anything or for it to be finished.

Cut moodiness.

Cut fear away.

Cut through all ideas about emptiness or void

And any bias towards non-existence as truth or a place of refuge.

There is nothing to rely on in concepts.

The profound simplicity of the guru's speech is the only guide.

Because this is the unending mandala of the battlefield

Which teems with crude and subtle enemies,

Cut again and again and again and again

As long as there is any thought or emotional conflict.

This is not discipline.

This is the sound and movement of naked prajna itself.

Do not lose heart."

Where the diamond sword had passed through each yogini's neck, only a line of blood the width of a hair, glowing like a blacksmith's fire, and filling the air with the red light of dawn marked its passage. Those who saw this were utterly dumbfounded. The sisters sang.

"There is no logic nor absence of logic,

No word nor absence of word

Nor existence nor non-existence.

Inexpressible,

Real without the opposition of unreality.

Moving without intention,

Free from obstruction,

Prajna is ceaseless.

Complexity is severed at the root.

This is the guru's spontaneous presence

Appearing from the continuity of prajna itself,

This is the empowerment of the damaru

From which all outer and inner phenomena emerge

As the vowels and consonants,

And of the kapala, the limitless natural container of all,

The ground of the deathless primordial union of guru and disciple."

From the two veins in the yoginis' necks, streams of red and white bodhicitta spurted out, curving through the air and, touching the outstretched tongues of the severed heads, poured in an unending stream into their gaping mouths.

"Cutting off all appearance of duality:

Wisdom and ignorance, form and emptiness,

Prajna, at one stroke,

Severs and reveals the life-essence of duality:

The stream of co-emergence,

The red and white elements of mother and father.

"Inseparable from them,

Prajna is the melting fire of union.

"Revealing and revealed by this union,

Prajna is the source of all.

The sustenance of all.

One taste.

Two I am one.

One I am two. "

2.iii

They offered their severed heads with bloodshot eyes glaring madly and black hair swirling upwards to the Great Guru. Kanha laughed and touched the forehead of each as a sign of his acceptance, as their song continued.

"Because there is no confirmation by any union,

I, Prajna am the consort.

I, Prajna am the lover and the end,

I am the embrace,

The final illusion called other.

I am the mind which moves

Without finding a place to dwell,

Without being a stable subject from which to project

Or experience any illusion.

And I am the creation of that mind.

I am the sought unfound,

The unfulfilled desired,

The never known.

I am the sacrifice of all that lives

Within the limits of life, death, desire and form

Moving always beyond all limit.

I am the origin and sustenance and end of all

Which moves and dwells within such limits.

And I am the sacrifice for all that lives.

I am the essence and heart,

Pouring out,

Sustaining, but not coursing in the limits

Of any form or body."

A deep turquoise light, the color of an autumn morning sky, emanated from their hearts and suffused all the air, while the sisters themselves seemed to flicker like a raging fire. The minds of all others who saw this were utterly paralyzed. The sight was unbearable, yet they could not take their eyes away.

"Exhilaration

Terror

I am the intensity of movement and presence.

There is no solidification by desire or concept.

Consumed in movement,

Filling all of space,

I am the absolute source and void.

Delirium filling all of space,

I am the intoxication of the thousand worlds."

Although there was complete silence, for those, immersed in blue light, staring at the fiery display, it seemed as if a deep melodious song pierced their marrow.

"Melting in my embrace,

This is the empowerment of Prajna-jnana,

The inseparability of ground and path:

Movement devoid of concept and emotional bias

Movement inseparable with motionless space.

The indissoluble union of mind and guru,

I am mind, pure without limit,

Without even the limit of a notion of mind.

Freed from any goal

Anger is insight not limited by knowing;

Pride is equanimity not limited by ownership;

Lust is love not limited by confirmation;

Envy is completion not limited by completeness.

I am the living pathway to the vajra world.

Since nothing is ever separable from me,

There is no end.

I am the heart."

3.i

Then the sisters Mehkala and Kanakhala, dancing backwards rose together into the sky on a bridge of light. As they rose, lights of every color radiated from their bodies, and the brilliance was such that it made all the sky and earth seem dark.

"Phenomena and space,

Relative and absolute truth,

Prajna and compassion,

The mandala of existence

And dharmadhatu itself

Are one in the boundary-less expanse of Kanha's stainless mind.

Free from any reference point whatsoever,

Unlimited action, ceaseless love,

Utterly unmoving,

Kanha is all the kayas in one being.

Surrendering into this,

Is not meditation.

Surrendering completely

Is the supreme prajna.

Ignorance and awareness,

Bondage and freedom are one.

Prajna is the all-pervasive light of phenomena,

The essence of space,

And space itself.

From the non-dual union of space and awareness,

The unborn bindu of blazing luminosity

Illuminates totality.

In shadowless complete surrender,

This is the vajra dance.

AH "

3.ii

Then the great lord, the Mahacarya Kanha, stretched forth his right
arm which extended effortlessly up into the center of space like a ray of
light. Taking the head of each in turn, he replaced it on the body so
that no scar or mark remained. He took both in his hand and brought
them to earth. He smiled at them and they went about their way.

To a melody like laughter, Kanha sang this song:

"Seeing it, it cannot be assimilated.

Remembering it, it cannot be known.

Thinking of it, no meaning can be found.

Describing it compounds uncertainty and misunderstanding.

Forgetting it, one is still haunted.

Thus it cannot be opposed."

In this manner, with the complete and self-existing dedication of merit, the great lord Kanha sealed the display of the All-Awakened One, The Sarva Buddha Dakini who is Vajrayogini and Prajnaparamita in person, the self-existing Dharmacakra.

SARVA SVABHAVA PRAJNA MANGALAM SVAHA

THE LIFE OF KING INDRABHUTI

In a dream, Gesar, King of Ling finds himself in Kusinagra, and sees, lying across a vast plain the enormous sleeping form of Mahaprabha, King of Suprabha. The glowing body of Mahaprabha, as Gesar sees, contains all the beings of all time, whether past, present or future. Some have lifespans that are measureless while others live only for an instant. Mahaprabha shimmers with life while all within him are impermanent, but for him there is no time. In Mahaprabha's body, regardless of what appears as fate and fortune, everything is inseparable from the magic of knowledge, the magic of intrinsic freedom, the magic of display. An old wrinkled servant appears and gives this text to Gesar, King of Ling.

*

THE SUN OF SOVEREIGNTY

INVOKING THE INNATE,

THE MAHASIDDHA BHUMIPALA,

KING INDRABHUTI THE GREAT

1

On the blazing surface of the cosmic mirror,

Billions of drops of gold amrita coalesce

And fall in galaxies of realms,

An unceasing rain of all-pervasive radiance;

Swirling free in the vastness of space,

This rain is mind, is sun and moon,

Is sky, is mountain, is perfume,

Is melody, is sea, is sex, is spice and wine.

Its luminosity is co-emergence.

Its heat is the union of prana and upaya.

Its power is kaya and jnana,

Embodiment and wisdom undivided at the core.

Thus the Imperial Yana which never departs,

Returns.

Thus the Imperial Yana, inseparable from phenomena

Is proclaimed.

Thus heaven and earth are inseparable.

2

Once King Indrabhuti sat in the cool of the day with his consorts and ministers on the terrace of his palace in Odiyana. He looked up into the early morning sky, and saw what appeared to be a great flock of scarlet cranes flying through the air. The king asked his ministers: "What are those birds? Where do they come from?"

"Your majesty, those are not birds at all, but Arhats in their red robes. They are the disciples of the Great Sage, the Buddha, the Fully Awakened One. It is said, sire, that by following the Buddha's teachings, his followers find release from the bonds of clinging that tie others to this world. Thus they may fly north and south to spread his teachings" The King considered this and then asked how he might meet the this great teacher. The ministers explained that the sage lived far away and was not likely to come such a great distance.

But when the Great King heard the name of the Awakened One, his heart melted with longing. And when the Buddha's name passed his lips, all thoughts in his mind stopped. He did not hear his minister's words, nor the talk of his wives. He sat unmoving as the sun set, the moon rose and set, and the sun rose once again. Wordlessly and silently, an ocean of pure awareness opened to King Indrabhuti and expanded like an all-embracing mirror.

3

Days later, the Arhats crossed the noon-day sky in a great migration that seemed like clouds at sunset. King Indrahuti called out to them. He asked how they could be so unconstrained by the laws of nature; by near and far, by high and low. They circled above him. King Indrabhuti could not tell if the words he heard were their reply or his own thoughts.

"Awareness simultaneously something and not;

Freedom from all qualities simultaneously something and not;

Mind simultaneously something and not;

Expanse of thoughts simultaneously something and not;

Taking sides in the snap of that instant,

Beings and realms are born and not.

But like an eternal sun

This simultaneity is origin and end.

This simultaneity itself

Is unborn all-pervasive radiance.

This Samaya of Mind

Is called the All Consuming."

4

Later King Indrabhuti sat in his palace shrine hall. His mind was filled with longing. Calling out for the 500 Arhat attendants of the Buddha, he set out a vast array of offerings: pure water, flowers, incense, hundreds of lamps, perfume and food. He commanded his musicians to play and sing the most beautiful melodies known to them.

Soon, swirling downward through the sky, the Arhats descended there like an immense flock of red birds, and as they sat before him, the Great King asked them to show him the direct path to enlightenment.

The Arhats then replied:

"Turn your mind from this mirage which is nothing but a prison and a torture house gaily painted like a palace to entrance and deceive. Renounce the world and find the path to the enlightenment which does not change."

Indrabhuti considered this in silence for a long time. He shook his head and as if seeing his palace and all around him for the first time, sang this song:

"Monks, you are indeed heroes and noble sons.

But I am a king, not a renunciant.

A great world surrounds me.

76

When the sun rises, I wake to see it.

When the moon rises and the stars shine,

I feel the tenderness of their cool breath.

When my people sing, a child cries, or my consort calls out in the night,

I hear them and my heart moves to them.

When I smell the lotus blooming on the lake

Or the smell of the smoke from the charnel ground, my mind is still.

When I am caressed, I am joyful,

And when I drink wine, I am filled with delight.

Surely, this is the breath of enlightenment

And the living heart-beat of the Awakened One."

The Arhats were speechless. Again King Indrabhuti sat on his throne without moving for a long time. Without moving, he surveyed the world of form as it arose from the mandala of the five lights. Those with him heard these words:

"In the distinction between kaya and jnana,

Embodiment and wisdom,

Beings grasp at recognition, partial recognition, and non-recognition;

Wisdom and illusion appear separate.

All the oceans of galaxies of realms arise."

Thus, King Indrabhuti's senses expanded effortlessly. Opening through infinite space, free from the limits of emotional bias or conceptual structures, King Indrabhuti saw the limitless ocean of galaxies of realms. These words were heard:

"In the seeming division of kaya and jnana,

Life itself and the life of realms and beings

Is Shila Samaya called The Inexhaustible."

5

King Indrabhuti sat before the Arhats on his throne, eating and drinking and smiling at his consorts, ministers, and generals, as at the same time he gazed on the infinity of realms and beings. Again the Great King asked the Arhats for the path to enlightenment which does not deny the realms of form. And again the Arhats answered:

"Oh Greatest of Kings, you must abandon all desire and craving. Cultivate morality, meditation and wisdom. Develop the Paramitas of generosity, discipline, patience, exertion, meditation and prajna."

The King replied: " I wish to see the direct path of complete wakefulness which does not abandon the delights of the five senses and the bliss I share with my consorts." And then he sang:

"Even if it be likely that one so attached to the senses as I

Be reborn a fox deep in the forests of my kingdom:

Oh Gautama I will realize enlightenment, the innate ground

Without surrendering the slightest passion for this world."

Then, King Indrabhuti reached out and took the hand of his consort.
As the rays of the sun fill all the sky and illuminate all the earth, it
seemed that King Indrabhuti embraced the entire world completely.

At that moment, some of King Indrabhuti's attendants and ministers
saw him as he sat before them as nothing other than a great cloud filled
with light; others saw him in the form of Vajradhara, still others saw
King Indrabhuti as the Lord of Secrets, and others yet as a Rigden
King enthroned in Kalapa.

So, in the centerless center of primordial space,

Like the sun resting at mid-heaven,

King Indrabhuti, the radiant, stood as Lord of the Mandala of
Existence,

King of Illusion and Protector of the Earth-ground.

Then The Great Earth Protector Lord proclaimed this:

"O, you who wander in the human realm,

On the paths of deluded ordinary beings,

On the path of those who simply hear the truth,

On the path of celibate renunciants, on the path of private realization,

Or on any other path known thus far

Whether pursuing methods of purification or union,

You struggle for liberation from bondage in samara's whirling coils.

However subtly,

You conceive of enlightenment as escape;

Conceive of the infinite expanse of wakefulness

As heaven and final resting place.

I, Indrabhuti proclaim that enlightenment is not beyond the world.

It is the primordial ground.

It is all-pervasive.

Unoriginated, it is the source.

Unceasing, it is extinction.

Without location, it is like space.

Its radiance is the pulse of all thoughts and concepts.

Its glamour is the power of all attachments.

Its energy is the life force of all illusory lives.

Its stability is the foundation of all realms.

It's freedom is the pure play of all phenomena.

Because it is empty, it is the feeling of unreality.

Because it is the ground, it is the feeling of reality.

Because it is subtle, there is the experience of confusion.

Because it is unceasing, there is the experience of meaning.

Because it is non-duality, it is complete compassion.

Because it is compassion, it is the truth and the innate law.

Logic does not capture or penetrate it.

Renunciation does not purify it.

Meditation does not stabilize it.

Behavior does not expand or diminish it.

It is reality itself and is not an attainment of any kind.

Therefore my path, the path of Indrabhuti, is the path of King.

It is the display of liberation

Which is myriad worlds,

Moves in those worlds,

And is inseparable from them.

My path is the display of liberation

Which is this world.

Moves in this world,

And is inseparable from it.

Looking on the vast array of space,

See the mandala of this world;

When you hear the cries and songs of countless beings here,

Smell their tired sweat and sweet perfumes,

Sense their terror, lust, and longing,

That seeing, hearing, smelling, touching, tasting,

That knowing

Makes those worlds, makes this world

Inseparably ours

And deeply to be loved.

So this world, for we who dwell here,

Is the co-emergent form of pure complete enlightenment.

Moving from realm to realm

By awareness, by vision, by living,

By caring for the well-being of every living being,

By loving them;

All this is the same as the light of the sun

Passing through clouds."

Then, as he sat before all his court, King Indrabhuti clasped his consort tightly to him. His consorts, ministers, generals and all his courtiers saw him enter into the vast and pulsing flow of time. He appeared to them riding on the back of a golden garuda flying through sky after sky, appearing in age after age, place after place, and form after form. He flashed through the swirling flow of cyclical illusions, sometimes entirely visible, sometimes in part, sometimes hidden and sometimes only glimpsed as a flicker, like a fish dancing in a golden stream.

6

i

So

Appearing as the seasons,

As gold, silver, copper, and iron wheels,

He is the succession of Chakravartin Emperors.

Moving through time, he rules in different forms

By virtue of holding a gold, silver, copper, or iron wheel.

As these wheels whirl through space,

They generate a river of sound

Which is the music of unfolding reality

And is audible to all within thousands of miles of its passage.

It draws the hearts of all who hear it

To the way of the true law,

And the establishment of enlightened society.

With the Golden Wheel, all his court moves effortlessly everywhere,

And all the phenomena of this world are synchronized.

Thus he is lord of the four continents.

As holder of the Silver Wheel,

He is lord of the three continents in the East, South and West,

Conquering them simply by advancing in their direction.

As holder of the Copper Wheel,

He becomes lord of the Eastern and Southern continents

Simply by preparing for battle.

As holder of the Iron Wheel,

He gains control of the Southern Continent

Simply by brandishing weapons.

All subsequent Chakravartin Emperors only rule a single continent.

Their virtues cause no jealousy or rivalry.

Appearing as the cycles of the sun throughout the year,

First he is Dawa Zangpo,

Renewing the request of King Indrabhuti,

And drawing out the Kalachakra from the Tathagata himself.

Then he displays all his aspects

As the succession of Lords of Shambhala.

Moving through time, he rules in different forms

As dharma unfolds in the form of a lotus.

Appearing as the phases of the moon,

He is each of the four ancestral sovereigns,

Ashoka Maharaja, Gesar King of Ling,

The Yung Lo Emperor, and Prince Shotoku Taishi.

Appearing as galaxies of moving stars,

He is a vast variety of just lords

Who leave great words and deeds, but have no successors.

iii

Appearing in the succession of the hours,

He is a stream of other Indrabhutis

Who are great Mahasiddhas,

Writing down the tantras,

In realm after realm, teaching and showing his subjects

The path of natural liberation,

Everywhere he is the consort of great dakinis.

Everywhere he begins and follows the lineage of teacher and disciple.

iv

And as, in the motionless darkness of the night

The sun seems suddenly to blaze out,

He is the eternal spontaneously arisen Earth Protector,

The Profound, Brilliant, Just, Powerful, All Victorious Sakyong.

Thus does King Indrabhuti hold the mudra samaya,

Called the Imperial One.

7

In the time when he was first spoken of, Indrabhuti gathered all the tantras together in book form and instructed all the people of Uddiyana. Thus his realm is a pure realm.

His mind, his practice and his actions were and are ever united and inseparable from the samayas of a Sakyong and all the samayas of all the tantras. Thus, he practices in one realm after the other, and all are realized as pure realms.

So it is said that at that time, King Indrabhuti together with all his consorts, all his attendants, every single one of his subjects including ghosts, animals, insects, fish and birds, attained the siddhi of rainbow body.

This great king did not consider his existence, his path and his enlightenment in any way separable from the countless beings in his realm. Detachment never stained his mind. His passion was a great sea vessel carrying all he encountered or knew of over oceans of suffering. His love is a sun that never sets.

This is the original life of King Indrabhuti the Great.

OM BHUMIPALA SVABHAVA SARVA MANGALA SVAHA

Gesar is lost in a blizzard and he sings this:

All Buddhas, infinite as snow flakes in a storm,

Bright as oceans of stars,

You dwell in all realms in whatever is called space.

You manifest in all eons in whatever is called time.

Infinite in form, you dance:

You share a single gesture.

You each produce illusion on illusion on illusion:

Rainbows within rainbows within rainbows.

You shine in an illusory sky,

Opening in the eyes and hearts of beings

In a living moment of self-liberated awake.

Gesar sings this song early one afternoon while walking by the Brahamaputra River:

1

Right where you are,

Transcending time and space,

Gesar, King of Ling, Lord of the Realms of Form,

Wearing the dazzling armor of noonday sun,

Carrying the full moon banner of exultation,

Swirling the star light sword of pure awareness,

Riding the miracle horse of universal life force,

Flies from moment to moment and shape to shape.

He is the Indestructible Warrior free from time.

Gesar is renewal itself.

He passes like wind through past, present, future.

Spontaneously he destroys what needs to be destroyed.

He binds anew the elements and times.

Ever moving, he weaves anew the senses.

Again, he cuts down the three lords of materialism.

Again and again, he conquers the Demon lords of passion,
aggression, ignorance.

Right where you are,

Transcending time and space.

You may lose heart; you do not see it.

The human world is cracking up.

A century of warfare, genocide, destruction and want

Has severed men and women from their roots.

They have no forbears, no folkways or culture, no past.

Money has shredded all other values.

The young wander in a phantasmagoria of luxurious diversions,

Violence, intoxication, constant novelty and hopelessness.

Elders are abandoned; whatever wisdom they might have found discarded.

Language has no more eloquence.

There is no ground.

All know

The earth will not long sustain this whirlwind of consumption.

Pollution and the fear of pollution are everywhere.

Everywhere people struggle to separate from the sickened earth.

Everywhere, they strive to avoid the fate of all,

Desperately amassing gilded walls of wealth,

Anxiously cultivating peaceful states of mind,

Smugly practicing religions that leave the world far behind.

The visions of humanity and the reality of earth are parting.

3

Swamped in the shriek and welter of materialistic cravings

The Buddha dharma is corrupted or inaudible.

The Buddha cuts through fear and craving;

Life and death, the myriad forms of universal love, consumed
him.

He taught the path of boundless love.

But now in the blinding roar of world delusion,

The door of light the Buddha opened to the world

Begins to close.

Now,

Now Gesar of Ling, the Unconquerable Warrior, leaves the world

Again he dissolves back into the world of myths and stories;

He returns to the great source,

The flow of feelings, thoughts, sensation

The great river of life.

Again

Right where you are,

Transcending time and space.

Gesar hears a voice, a heartbeat.

He is poised on the edge of a new world.

He enters a new world and new time.

Again

Right where you are,

Transcending time and space.

Now Gesar, the Perfect Warrior, wakes

In the silent pause

Of searching for a word,

A world recalled by the scent of a catalpa tree in bloom,

Searching for a word that brings a question into being

That finds a riddle answered

A world on the horizon of being born.

Right where you are,

Transcending time and space.

Gesar, King of Ling turns back into legend.

He dissolves himself further into the ancient words,

The ancient time, the ancient stream. the ancient sagas,

He wanders on the timeless path.

He renews dharma in the timeless stream.

Now

Right where you are,

Transcending time and space.

Now,

Riding on the breath of life,

Gesar enters the past and emerges from the past.

He flies like a silver arrow

Into the tumultuous sky of illusion.

Instant by instant,

Without any intent,

He reinvents the world.

II

VISIONS AND SONGS

OF GESAR, KING OF LING

*

THE MIRROR OF NOWNESS:

THE LEGACY

OF THE RULERS OF

SHAMBHALA

II. 1

Gesar, King of Ling, Destroyer of Demons, makes his way home at the head of his army. They wind their way along rocky riverbeds and rise onto steep mountain trails. When they reach the summit of the first mountain pass, they see before them rank upon rank of jagged snow mountains amid billowing white cloud banks ranged before them. They pause, awe-struck as if they are on the border of a different world. Gesar laughs and sings to them, beginning with some verses from the Avatamsaka Sutra:

"The Flower Bank Ocean of worlds

Expands further than the universe.

Pure, it is pure in every sense;

At peace, peace, it fills all of space.

In this ocean of worlds

Are more world systems than any mind conceives.

Each is arrayed in different shapes, colors, senses.

Each is utterly independent.

They cannot be mistaken, one for the other.

Like networks of cities,

They circle each other like whirlpools,

Like vast blooming lotus flowers."

*

II.1

THE COSMIC MIRROR

1

In the all-pervasive pure immensity of primordial space,

The limitless, the timeless;

Space before stillness, time before occurrence,

The signless, the directionless, the gateless;

In this realm which neither appears nor disappears;

Space without other, ground without path, the primordial mandala

Is pure presence, is pure reality itself.

Now,

Without beginning,

Now,

Without end,

The cosmic mirror

Is the spontaneous expanse of infinite space.

The first moment without the second,

The cosmic mirror is primordial nowness.

Now,

Radiating within the space beyond space and the time beyond time,

Everywhere and simultaneously.

Now,

Light before illumination and shadow;

Luminosity inseparable from bliss,

The radiance of all, bliss of all,

The self-luminous blazes as gates of light.

Now,

Without logic or consequence,

Sight, sound smell, taste and touch

Shine

Free from the limits of perceiver, perception or consciousness.

This is the all-encompassing radiance

Of the cosmic mirror.

3

Now,

As a bolt of lightning, as a sharp cry

All the wisdom of the cosmic mirror

Condenses.

A sudden dot,

Vibrant, alive, awake,

Pulses in the infinite expanse of luminous space.

Now is the all-pervasive life

Of vision, tenderness and courage.

The Kingdom of Shambhala

Rises beyond time

Complete, brilliant and all-pervasive

In every instant.

THE BRILLIANT SUCCESSION OF THE LORDS OF KALAPA:

II.2

THE KINGDOM OF SHAMBHALA

As the sun rises, gilding the mountain granite peaks and touching the billowing clouds with the tint of pink lotuses, Gesar wakes, and sings out:

"Flames of crystal from the sea,

Inconceivable nets of light,

World systems like this,

Float on lotus blossoms."

He laughs and continues:

Floating on the radiance of nowness

In the infinite circle of the cosmic mirror,

The Kingdom of Shambhala appears as a pure realm.

The Kingdom of Shambhala appears on the face of this earth.

The Kingdom of Shambhala appears as the secret form of the human heart.

Because Shambhala is nowness,

It is all-pervasive as basic goodness.

Because Shambhala does not rely on confirmation,

It expands as the vastness of the ayatanas.

Because Shambhala vaults over the apparent opposition of phenomena,

It rises as the power of wind horse.

Because Shambhala is timeless.

It is always appropriate.

Because Shambhala is self-fulfilling,

It is awake in the primordial stroke.

It possesses the spontaneous confidence of Lion, Tiger, Garuda, Dragon.

2

Luminous, immense, verdant, stately and eternal,

The Kingdom of Shambhala is hidden.

A towering range of impenetrable, glistening snow-mountains,

Formed from time

Frozen by the anger, lust and ignorance of egoistic fixation,

Completely surrounds it.

Within this circular ice mountain wall,

The Kingdom of Shambhala, "Held by the Source of Happiness", opens

In the shape of vast lotus with eight petals.

The melting waters of Shambhala's mountains

Form eight cold blue racing streams

Which enrich its fields and forests

And mark the boundaries of the Kingdom's eight provinces.

In each province, farms, forests, lakes and towns

Adorn the land, as dew in sunlight

Sparkles on a lotus' outstretched petals.

This is the land where the intrinsic sacredness

Of humanity has never been lost,

And is always whole.

The births of all who dwell here are free of pain.

Following the ways of their ancestors and the guidance of elders,

They are raised according to the inner path of meditation,

And cultivate the outer paths of art and warrior discipline.

Their manner is dignified, direct and considerate,

And their lives are untouched by sickness, hunger, unhappiness
or poverty.

Both men and women are true warriors,

But live the lives of ordinary householders.

Their lives span a hundred years,

And they view their deaths with equanimity

As no different from the transitions of life. (1,2)

Their confidence and kindness

Appear in the ordinary human realm

As galaxies of stars in the dark of night.

In each province, as on the apex of a lotus petal's gentle curve,

Sits a glittering capital city.

In the east is The Proud One; in the southeast, The Vast Field;

In the south, the Secret; in the west, The Flexible One;

In the northwest, The Happy One; in the north, The Originating
One;

And in the northeast, The Radiant One.

In the gleaming inner courts of these capitals

Reside the Lords of Shambhala,

The father and mother lineages of dralas.

Their minds do not stray from nowness.

They are gentle and fearless.

By speech and symbol,

They expand the luminous, vast perception of nowness

Unrestricted by the limits of conventional thought.

Their brilliance blazes through the realm of human time

As protectors, as mountain gods and goddesses of lakes,

As non-dual sudden wakefulness.

THE KALAPA COURT

As the sun moves to mid-heaven and all is blinding brightness, Gesar sings out:

"The glittering webs of light in every universe

Can never be described,

But are the gates to every land,

The gates of mystery and wonder."

*

At the center of the Kingdom of Shambhala,

Like silver anthers rising amid golden lotus petals,

A towering ring of crystal mountains rises

Formed from time frozen by concepts of eternalism and nihilism.

Theses glittering peaks surround a lofty circular green plateau,

The great park of Malaya, adorned with turquoise lakes and
crystal streams.

Glades of juniper, tamarisk, bamboo and rhododendron perfume
the air.

Here stands the mandala of Kalachakra,

Surrounded by the mandalas of the eight gods, the eight Naga kings,

The protectors of the ten directions,

The nine great destroyers, the gods of the eight planets,

The twenty-eight stars, and innumerable other protector deities.

At the center of Malaya, arising in the spontaneous heart of nowness,

Is the ultimate court of primordial time,

Kalapa, "The Timely", the capital of Shambhala,

Glowing with an intense radiance that fills the whole of space.

Here dwell the Earth Protectors and Rigdens

Who rule over all Shambhala

And radiate the heart of all true human law.

Kalapa is a vast square with high bright ruby walls

Surmounted by golden balustrades.

Its four gates are made from sapphire, yellow diamond, ruby and emerald.

Within the walls are the inner gates and courtyards paved with white opal.

In the center, on a platform of pearl, is a great palace, the Kalapa Court.

It is made of gold and looms nine stories high

With pillars and beams made of cinnabar, silver, coral and gzi.

Its floors are ebony, sandalwood and cedar.

It's moldings are made of silver and liquid gold,

And its roof and the floor of its throne room

Are made from crystal plates that radiate heat.

Its roof is surmounted by victory banners and a gold
dharmachakra.

Garlands of gold and pearl hang from its eaves.

The luster of the palace is so great that it dims the sun and moon,

And the sky above the palace shines like a sparkling sea.

Also within the ruby walls of Kalapa, surrounding the central
palace

Are thirty-one smaller pavilions built in the same way.

Each is surrounded by gardens and streams.

The sound of chimes and the scent of flowers fill the air.

Here dwell the Rulers of Shambhala,

The seven Earth Protector Dharma Rajahs and twenty-five
Rigdens.

The Rulers of Shambhala appear directly from the heart of the
cosmic mirror

As nowness pervades the endless succession of time.

As timelessness pierces the endless stream of cause and effect,

The rulers of Shambhala follow one after another

Just as the sun moves across the sky.

Thus primordial time radiates within the realm of time

As ruler, as guide, as sustenance, as vision.

2

Inseparable from the fabric of the vast and minute cycles of time itself,

The thirty-two Lords of Kalapa

Move slowly across the luminous court yard.

Each in turn dwells in each of the thirty-two pavilions of Kalapa.

Each in succession appears in rulership,

Resolving, one into the other,

As the many rays and aspects resolve into a single blazing sun.

The True Law of the human realm

Resounds with their foot-fall.

Time unfolds as the vowels and consonants

Weave the binding of the senses and elements

To the pervasive unwavering blue light of Samantabhadra.

Thus the mind of the rulers shines in light.

The mood of their command colors the sky.

Their deeds are the dance of the elements.

The sun and moon are their wisdom display,

The stars and planets show their path,

The four seasons are their law

In order that confidence blaze like a prairie fire

In the hearts of all men, women and children.

In order to show the law inherent in the movements of the
human,

The Lords of Kalapa, the Rulers of Shambhala

Appear in the Kalapa Court,

One after the other;

Appear in slow procession

And the whole of time resounds from their footsteps.

So

Through the blessings of the elements and ayatanas,

The Kingdom of Shambhala appears

As living reality on the very face of this earth,

Alive in every breath, sound, mood, season,

Hour and instant.

*

DHARMA RAJAH SUCANDRA

Now, as Gesar and his warriors traversed the high mountains and plains, it was as if they were traveling in a magic land. Gesar sang to them, recounting the lineage of the Rulers of the Kingdom of Shambhala, the enlightened pure land that is far to the North. He began with some more verses from the miraculous Avatamsaka sutra:

"The Mind-King Jewel

Appears in different colors to different minds,

But when a mind is unclouded by hope and fear,

The pure lands can be clearly seen.

Like great Dragon Kings

Creating clouds that fill the sky,

The power of an enlightened ruler's vow

Brings joy and virtue to his land."

With these verses he began this long song:

The Earth Protector Kings

Who ruled the land called Shambhala,

Which means 'Held by the Source of Happiness',

Were all descended from Shambhaka of the Sakya clan,

Emerging from this immemorial lineage,

Sucandra, Auspicious Moon, the Lord of Secrets,

Is the first to be called a Dharma King.

Now he enters the Crystal Hall of the Kalapa Court.

This great Dharma Raja enters this world as an emanation of Vajrapani,

The All-Conquering Lord of Secrets,

Who brings the blazing light of wisdom

Into the fickle realities of the human realm.

Vajrapani is the master of Buddha Activity

Beyond the waxing and waning of life and death.

Out of Vajrapani's heart, the Dharma King Sucandra takes birth

As the first son of King Suryaprabha and Queen Vijaya.

Thus he enters the Kalapa Court and takes his seat on the Lion Throne.

His pale face is serene and his dark gaze fathomless.

His hair and mustache are black and smooth.

He wears the Gold Crown of Reality Beyond the Limit of Knowledge

Which is surmounted by a white diamond free of any flaw.

As the lord of heart and mind,

He wears gold earrings shaped like sea-dragons.

His dragon-patterned brocade robe is turquoise.

His sash is pale red like an early winter moon.

In his right hand he holds a white lotus

On which stands a crystal Vajra;

In his left a silver bell.

He sits on a glowing golden throne

Beneath the rainbow-colored parasol of complete fearlessness

Which is vast as the sky and supported by a golden pole high as Mount Meru.

Encountering him is overwhelming

As if one had emerged in the night from a narrow mountain pass

And found oneself suddenly on an immense plain bathed in full moonlight.

In his unchanging secret form, the Great Dharma King Sucandra

Is ever youthful and his body is white as a conch.

His face is inviting and completely peaceful.

Because he has attained the summit of dharma,

His top-knot is surmounted by the three jewels,

Each blazing from its own inner radiance.

He wears the flower garland crown of the five senses

And a necklace of the five elements displayed as five kinds of gem-stones.

He wears a red and gold brocade shawl as radiant as the splendor of love.

His golden bracelets are the four aims of life.

He wears the Jewel Treasure of the Ocean on a gold chain at his heart.

In his right hand, he holds the Wish Fulfilling Tree,

And in his left a red lotus,

On which stands the golden eight-spoked wheel of unobstructed truth

Surmounted by the three jewels.

His consort on his right, gold as the dawn sun,

Makes the gesture of timeless offering,

Extending the gold vase of eternal life surmounted by the flaming three jewels.

The Dharma King Sucandra is surrounded

By all the offerings of the phenomenal world.

In the peace of his radiance, there is no room for doubt or discursiveness.

3

The Great Dharma Raja Sucandra journeyed to the stupa of Dhyanakataka,

Accompanied by a great retinue of Nagas, Dralas,

And a vast number of his own subjects.

There the Great Lord prostrated to the Enlightened One,

Sage of the Sakyas, the Gautama Buddha,

The conqueror of the three worlds and light of this age.

The Dharma Raja requested the teachings for one who remains a King,

Remains in the embrace of the senses, and seeks the well-being of all.

He requested the teachings that unfold outer life as an inner path.

He requested the teachings that open the gate of the seventh consciousness,

And purify the full display of the ayatanas.

He requested the teachings that show the world of Basic Goodness

Glowing and fertile in the light of the Great Eastern Sun.

According to the text of The Supreme First Buddha,

The way in which he made his request is told as follows:

To eliminate the kleshas of sentient beings

By the union of body, speech and mind,

He supplicated the Bhagavan by offerings

Of jewel flowers strewn at his lotus feet.

He supplicated with the petals of precious flowers,

With prostrations made on bended knee.

With right knee to the floor

And with palms joined at the forehead,

The Lord of Shambhala requested:

"The Unsurpassed Highest Tantra, The First Buddha

Gathers all siddhis, possesses the vowels and consonants,

The Glorious Yoga of Kalachakra

Instantly manifests perfect Buddhahood.

"Possessing the four times

By its 60 divisions,

It holds the four bindus:

The emptiness and wisdom bindu,

The great supreme Vajra Holder,

The great emptiness of five words,

The empty bindu of six letters.

"Outer, body, Buddha, god, and non-god, 25 classes of beings,

All are within the nature

With bodies of various scale

Which are the cause of the three worlds' arising,

The enjoyment of gods and non-gods;

All these without exception

I ask the teacher to explain."   (2)

The interior of the stupa became an immeasurable skull cup,

The inconceivable expanse of the dharmadhatu.

There, in the infinite expanse without beginning or end,

The Buddha arose in the form of Vajrasattva

And opened the mandala of Kalachakra, The Lord of Time.

In the great dance of Vajra compassion,

He opened the immeasurable palace:

Below, he displayed the twelve blissful aspects

Of the Lord of Vajradhatu Speech;

Above, he displayed the sixteen mandalas of stars.

All this had not been seen, heard or known

Since the eon of Buddha Dipankara.

In this way, the Buddha himself gave the initiation

Into the great Mandala of Vajradhatu

And conveyed the root text of the Tantra of Glorious Kalachakra.

The Root Tantra explains the essence:

Ka is pacification of cause.

La is dissolving.

Cha is the motion of mind.

Kra is being bound to the stages.

And the Great Commentary expands this:

Whoever has neither cause nor characteristics,

Is without movement and free from stages:

This is the meaning of Kalachakra.

To that non-duality, I make homage.   (3)

Returning to Shambhala, Dharma Raja Sucandra

Recorded all this in writing, the "Paramadibuddha" in 12,000 verses,

With commentary five times that length.

Upon returning to Kalapa,

 Dharma King Sucandra manifested his pure perception

As a great pleasure garden

To the south of the Palace of Kalapa and to the West of the "Near Lake".

In the midst of that vast park called Malaya,

From liquid gold, rubies, sapphires, emeralds,

Crystal, coral, and turquoise and silver,

The Dharma Lord built the great Body Mandala of the Lord of Time,

A perfect square with four gates, four arches and eight charnel grounds

With five surrounding fences,

And beyond them the mandala of the elements adorned with vajra chains.

Near it he built the Speech Mandala of Kalachakra, alike in form,

And close to that, he built the Mind Mandala of Kalachakra,

Alike in form but with three surrounding fences.

Closer still, he placed the Wisdom Mandala of Kalachakra

Surrounded by sixteen jeweled towers.

Again nearest yet to the Kalapa Court, the Dharma King Sucandra

Created a vast eight-petalled lotus

Whose golden anthers sway on breezes of delight and brush the sky,

Radiating like a hundred suns.

Placed in the timeless expanse of pure perception

The Mandalas of the Lord of Time are utterly complete

In every aspect and characteristic and power.

From this moment on, time is marked with the names of the Kings of Kalapa.

It is from this time that the names of the Lords of Kalapa are known to all.

It is from this time that the teachings of Shambhala flourish,

Blazing through all the human realm and in every human heart.

*

THE BRILLIANT SUCCESSION OF THE LORDS OF KALAPA

II.4.2

DHARMA RAJAH SURESVARA

1

Now the second Dharma Rajah enters the Crystal Hall of the Kalapa Court.

He is Dharma Raja Suresvara, Lord of Asuras,

Binding All Beings by Love in Union with Pure Nowness.

The great Dharma King Suresvara enters this world

As an emanation of Bodhisattva Kshitigharbha,

Who, because he loves all living beings as if he were their mother,

Is called:The 'Womb of Earth'.

Kshitigharbha appears as a simple monk.

The mark of perfection shines on his forehead.

He holds the wish-fulfilling gem in his right hand.

Because his love supports all beings in the six realms,

He holds in his left hand, a staff with six rings.

Determined that none who are born shall linger in the bonds of suffering,

He is the protector of all children

And carries a child in the crook of his right arm.

He is the compassion of the Buddha,

Inseparable from every form of life,

The final liberator of all who suffer all the tortures of hell.

2

Ruling from within the Crystal Palace, the Dharma Lord Suresvara

Sits at ease beside the wish-fulfilling tree

In a garden filled with fragrant trees.

His face is ruddy and his expression is determined and loving.

His hair and mustache are black and oiled.

He wears the gold crown of a dharma king

Surmounted by a ruby that glows like a dawn sun.

He wears a vermilion brocade robe adorned with gold garudas.

His sash is white as winter ocean spray.

He wears the gold necklaces, earrings and bracelets of an earth-protector.

In his right hand, he holds the gold Vajra prod

Which guides the mad elephant of mind

Through the jungles of claustrophobia and aggression,

In his left hand, he holds a rope of iron

Which draws all beings out of hell

With the ring of faith and hook of longing.

The sight of him overcomes all chaos, uncertainty, and anger

And one experiences complete confidence in the power of unconditional love.

3

In his unchanging secret form, the Dharma Raja Suresvara

Is dark red in color like heart's blood.

Youthful, naked to the waist,

He smiles and the sweetness of his expression pervades all space

Like the scent of honey suckle on a summer night.

He wears a crown of pink utpala flowers

And a scarf the color of laurel leaves.

He wears red pants and a skirt of blue brocade

Adorned with golden swirling clouds.

Because all aspects of the world are dear to him,

His body is adorned with gold necklaces.

And his arms with gold bracelets.

He sits on a throne before the coral and crystal gold-roofed palace of Kalapa

On a throne surmounted by the three jewels.

With his raised right hand, he plays an ivory damaru,

From which emerge all the vowels and consonants.

Thus all the senses vibrate in pure nowness.

In his left hand he holds a lotus the color of dawn

On which stands the blue jewel of the Buddha-nature itself,

Glowing amid the gold flames of all-consuming compassion.

His consort, gentle and white as a noon-day cloud,

Sits next to him holding the sun-disc of the complete power of mind.

*

DHARMA RAJAH TEJIN

1

Now the third Dharma Raja of Shambhala

Takes his seat within the Crystal Palace of the Kalapa Court:

He is Tejin, Glowing with the Splendor and Dignity of
Unconditional Confidence,

The bearer of the dharma wheel and auspicious conch.

The Dharma Raja Tejin enters this world as an emanation

Of the terrifying Conqueror and Lord of Death, Yamantaka.

Yamanataka is dark blue in color with thirty-four arms, sixteen
legs and nine heads,

His principal face is that of enraged buffalo.

His three blood-shot eyes wheel madly,

And below his burning snout his pointed iron teeth gnash.

He is adorned by serpents and garlands of human heads.

Because he sees to the core of all the cycles of time,

The empty radiance of reality itself.

The Dharma Lord Tejin sits erect near a fresh stream in a forest glade.

His face is dark brown and stern. His gaze is uncompromising.

His hair and mustache are black and cool.

He wears the gold crown of a dharma king, surmounted by a yellow diamond

Which shines like the sun appearing through the smoke of a battle-field.

He wears a glistening white robe embroidered with golden lions.

His sash is orange like an early sun.

He wears the gold necklaces, earrings and bracelets of an earth-protector.

In his right hand, he holds a golden eight-spoked dharma-chakra,

And in his left he holds a conch shell.

Thus he proclaims the unceasing path of liberation

And the truth which is not limited by words.

To see him is to experience a terror that cuts to the marrow,

As all one's self-absorption, one's schemes for self-satisfied happiness

Are revealed as cowardly vain, and finally fatal self-deceptions.

3

In his unchanging secret form, the Dharma Raja Tejin

Is the color of a lake of molten gold,

And he is youthful, naked to the waist.

His teeth are clenched,

And his three eyes stare implacably into the depths of space.

He wears the crown of the five families of Thatagathas,

And his red hair, the color of fire, is bound into a top-knot.

As the lord who is unaltered by time's endless cycles

And is never confused by changing reference points,

Blue serpents twine around his neck, wrists and ankles as
ornaments.

His legs are covered by a silk rainbow and he wears a tiger-skin
skirt.

In his raised right hand he upholds that which never changes,

The golden eight-spoked dharma chakra;

In his left hand he holds a pure white conch

Whose turnings shape the elements in ever shifting forms

And whose sound is the birth-cry of all creation.

His throne is a black and red jeweled palace

Floating amid clouds and a halo of time-ending fire,

And supported from below by three blue and two bronze water
buffalo.

His consort, on his right, is the color of pure lapis,

She holds the kapala of amrita which overcomes death

By dissolving belief in the permanence of individual existence

And the hooked knife which returns all thoughts to the essence.

*

THE BRILLIANT SUCCESSION OF THE LODS OF KALAPA

II.4.4

DHARMA RAJAH SOMADATTA

1

Somadatta, Gift of the Amrita Moon, The Lord of Speech,

Now enters the Crystal Palace of the Kalapa Court.

He is the fourth Dharma Raja of Shambhala.

Dharma Raja Somadatta enters this world as an emanation

Of the transcendent Bodhisattva

Sarvanivaranavikrambhin, the Conqueror of All Hindrances.

Sarvanivaranavikrambhin is pale blue like a summer moon

He is very young and his smile is inviting.

He holds in his right hand a white lotus.

On it, as if floating in the sky, the full moon of compassion
shines.

His left hand makes the gesture that overcomes all fear

And opens the moonlit path of self-existing fulfillment.

2

The Dharma Lord Somadatta sits on a throne on a high
mountain peak.

His face is the color of pearl. His gaze is passionate.

His hair and mustache are fine and black.

He wears the gold crown of a dharma king surmounted by a
moonstone

Whose soft luster fills the sky at evening.

He wears a robe of pale orange brocade marked with mating
tigers.

His silk sash is turquoise like a summer sea.

He wears the gold necklaces, earrings and bracelets of an earth-
protector.

In his right hand he holds the iron mace, the power of time

Which intoxicates and stupefies the mind, and breaks all who oppose it.

In his left hand he holds the diamond chains that bind the three worlds to nowness.

Thus he floods the world with a moon ocean of bliss, luminosity and complete non-thought.

To stand before him is to feel shy and eager like a passionate virgin

Meeting a lover for the very first time.

3

In his unchanging secret form, the Dharma Raja Somadatta

Is the all-pervasive blue-black color of midnight.

His teeth are clenched in a fierce smile,

And his three eyes gaze passionately into all phenomena.

He is the lord who exhausts all hunger and fulfills all thirsts.

He wears the crown of the five families of thataghatas.

And a halo of ruby light shines all around him.

He wears a heavy crimson robe embroidered in gold with coils of joy.

Beneath that he wears a white under-robe covered with silver clouds.

He sits on a red throne, and his left foot rests on a lotus and moon disc.

He holds in his raised right hand the flaming vajra sword

Cutting through the obsessions of all-consuming need.

In his left hand, he holds the golden shield,

The self-existing satiety of the mind of nowness.

His golden consort holds a fan adorned with blue peacock's feathers,

The sign of endless and uninterrupted offering,

The love that ends the tortured cravings of beings.

*

THE BRILLIANT SUCCESSION OF THE LORDS OF KALAPA
II.4.5

DHARMA RAJAH SURESVARA II

1

Now the fifth Dharma Raja of Shambhala,

The second to be named, Suresvara, Lord of Asuras,

The Destroyer of the Cities of Delusion,

Rules from the Crystal Palace of the Kalapa Court.

Dharma Raja Suresvara enters this world as an emanation

Of the self-born lord of ceaseless wrath, The Vajrakumara Vajrakilaya.

Vajrakilaya's towering body is radiant black.

He has three heads and six arms.

In his two central hands, he rolls a kila of meteoric iron

Whose top pierces the summit of the sky

And whose point penetrates the depth of existence.

In his embrace he holds his consort, pale blue as snow in moonlight.

Together, they blaze with all-consuming bliss.

This is the utter inseparability of space and awareness,

The primordial freedom that cuts through liberation.

2

The Dharma Lord Suresvara appears in the center of a field of flowers

Where he sits on the earth beside a treasure vase, amid fragrant blossoms.

His face is pale gold and his expression is still and thoughtful

As if he is looking into the ebb and flow of time.

His hair and mustache are black and cool.

He wears the gold crown of a Dharma King

Surmounted by an emerald which radiates black light.

He wears a gold brocade robe adorned with springing tigers.

His sash is dark blue as a clear autumn sky.

He wears the gold necklaces, earrings and bracelets of an earth-protector.

In his right hand, he holds a golden arrow with red garuda feathers and an obsidian tip

Which pierces space and opens the display of the sense fields.

In his left hand, he holds a bow made from the leg of a black antelope,

The power of yearning that projects all the realms of life and death.

Without concern, he fingers these great weapons as playthings,

And one feels paralyzed in his presence,

Full to the brim and completely empty.

3

In his unchanging secret form, the Dharma Raja Suresvara

Is glowing red like the all-consuming fire of time,

Youthful, radiant, naked to the waist.

He smiles, but his gaze is unmoving and fearless.

Because all aspects of the world are inseparable from his being,

He wears a crown of unconditioned love made from pink utpala flowers.

He wears swirling red silk pants and a skirt of blue brocade

Adorned with gold blazing clouds of flame.

His body is adorned with golden necklaces,

And his arms with gold bracelets, and a scarf the color of laurel leaves.

He sits before his fiery palace

On a burning throne surmounted by the three jewels.

With his raised right hand, he plays an ivory damaru,

From which emerge the vowels and consonants of creation and destruction,

Filling the whole of space.

In his left hand he holds a lotus the color of dawn

On which stands the blue jewel of the Buddha-nature itself,

Glowing amid the gold flames of totality.

His consort, still and white as a cloudless noon sky,

Sits next to him holding the sun-disc

In which all the myriad displays of mind unfold and fade.

*

DHARMA RAJAH VISVAMURTI

1

Now the sixth Dharma Raja of Shambhala,

Visvamurti, He Whose Form is the Universe,

The Conqueror of False Leaders, The Holder of The Imperial Lotus,

Enters the Crystal Pavilion of the Kalapa Court.

The great Dharma King enters this world,

As an emanation of the Sun of Nowness.

2

The Dharma Raja Visvamurti appears on a porch in a high mountain valley

Where he sits leaning on a laquer table piled high with texts.

A crystal and gold long life vase is on a table at his left.

His skin is white as fresh snow. He is youthful and his face is smooth.

He is poised like a young lion, waiting for the moment of command.

He wears the gold brocade turban and gold crown of a dharma king

Surmounted by a clear crystal that radiates cold morning light.

He wears a white brocade robe embroidered with lion cubs.

His sash is gold as sunlight reflected off of ice.

He wears the gold necklaces, earrings and bracelets of an earth-protector.

In his right hand which hangs loosely down,

He holds the golden Vajra ax whose blade of meteoric iron

Cuts the root of self-perpetuating ignorance.

In his left hand, which rests in his lap, he holds a text bound in red gold

Which is like a mirror to all the worlds that have been and yet shall be.

To encounter him is to experience great uncertainty.

As if one came across a young bull elephant grazing in a forest glade,

Ways to escape rush to mind, but one is awed by splendor.

3

In his unchanging secret form, the Dharma Raja Visvamurti

Is white as star light and all-pervasive as air,

Youthful, vibrant, naked to the waist.

His three eyes look fixedly into the primordial mirror.

His expression is implacable, and his gaze unwavering

As the changing shapes of life and time swirl before him.

He wears the crown of the five families,

And his red hair billows behind him like an autumn sunset.

His body is adorned with bracelets and necklaces,

With the serpent garlands of the unborn alaya

And a wreath of red utpala flowers of the purified ayatanas.

In his right hand he holds a golden vajra ax

Which cuts like lightening through the welter of discursive thought.

In his left, he offers a vast pink lotus in its first bloom,

As compassion expands without effort in the immensity of primordial awareness.

He wears pants of red brocade adorned with gold chrysanthemums.

He sits on a high red lacquer throne on a cushion of blue silk

Woven in the pattern of the eternal knot of meditation.

His right foot rests on the golden lotus

Which dispels all the poverty of ego fixation.

Beneath his throne is curled a male tiger with fierce wary eyes.

His consort at his left is the great yogini,

Red, naked with a tiger skin round her waist.

She wears the crown of the five families.

Bliss radiates through space as she plays the damaru in her right hand.

With her left hand, she offers the great lord a kapala of amrita

Which intoxicates the mind of birth and death.

*

THE BRILLIANT SUCCESSION OF THE LORDS OF KALAPA

DHARMA RAJAH SURESANA

1

Now the seventh Dharma Raja of Shambhala,

Suresana, He Who Rules and Possesses The Glory of the Gods

Dwells within the Crystal Pavilion of the Kalapa Court.

The great Dharma Rajah Suresana enters this world as an emanation

Of Bodhisattva Akashgharba, "Womb of Space".

Akashagharba's body is golden, and he wears a simple white silk robe.

He is youthful and sits at ease on a vast white lotus.

His face is peaceful and smiling.

He holds a small rainbow-colored jewel at his heart

From which light rays of compassion in every shade and hue

Radiate to fill the whole of space with the warmth of limitless love

And the light of unobstructed wisdom.

He is the offering which will never cease.

2

The Dharma Lord Suresana sits in a blazing mass of white light

On a crystal throne draped with lion skin.

His skin is the color of dark honey. His depthless black eyes shine,

And his thick red lips are parted in a smile.

His hair and mustache are long and perfumed.

He wears the gold brocade turban and gold crown of a dharma king

Surmounted by an obsidian which seems to pulse and vibrate.

He wears a red brocade robe embroidered with silver garudas.

His sash is white and sparkling as a mountain snow-cap.

He wears the gold necklaces, earrings and bracelets of an earth-protector.

Because of his completely pure samaya

Every movement of his mind self-liberates delusion,

So in his right hand, he holds the blazing vajra sword.

Because he turns all phenomena to bliss-emptiness,

In his left hand, he holds a gold and silver shield shaped like a coil of joy.

3

As if one stood before a benefactor offering a huge heap of jewels,

Encountering him one experiences oneself as stiff, pompous,

Humorless, rigid and self-righteous.   3

In his unchanging inner form, the Dharma Raja Suresana

Is deep blue as a boundless night without moon or stars.

His eyes look out like silver crescent knives.

His vivid expression has no quality whatsoever.

Because his mind has never moved,

He is the complete master of the three worlds:

Thus his hair is tied up into a three-tiered top-knot.

Because all temporary phenomena of birth and death are completely pure,

He wears crown and necklace of red and white lotuses.

In his right hand, he holds a lotus on which rests the hooked knife

Which spontaneously cuts through all solidifications

And in his left, he holds a lotus on which rests the kapala of amrita

Which completely intoxicates all duality.

The sea-colored gem whose radiance is every form of consciousness

Hangs on a gold chain at his heart.

He wears a dark blue robe embroidered with gold clouds,

And crimson silk trousers embroidered with the sun and moon.

His throne is a red gilded chariot wider than the universe,

Drawn across the whole of time by four furious blue stallions.

On his right, Queen Vishvamata, golden, radiant with every quality,

Offers on a golden tray a galaxy of jewels,

And, in a golden vase, the water of immortality.

*

DHARMA RAJAH AND FIRST RIGDEN

MANJUSRIKIRTI-YASAS

1

Now the eighth Dharma Raja of Shambhala, Manjusrikirti-Yasas,

The Renowned Friend of Manjusri,

Assumes the throne in the Crystal Pavilion of the Kalapa Court.

It is he who unites all the castes of Shambhala

In a single indestructible caste.

Thus he becomes the first Rigden.

The Dharma Lord Manjusrikirti-Yasas enters this world

As the emanation of Bodhisattva Manjusri, the Soft Voiced Lord,

The all-encompassing wisdom mind of complete wakefulness.

2

And in his secret unchanging nature,

Manjusrikirti Yasas retains the form of Manjusri.

His body is red, the color of a glowing ember.

His mind encompasses all that can be known and all that is beyond knowing.

In his soft smile, there is not the slightest hint of separation from anything.

He wears the jeweled crown of the five Thatagathas,

And in his top-knot is braided a gold five-pointed vajra.

His body is naked to the waist and adorned with the necklaces,

Bracelets and earrings of complete power over phenomena.

He wears red pants and a sky blue skirt embroidered with stars.

In his right hand, he holds the stem of a lotus

On which rests the blazing vajra sword which severs ignorance at the root.

In his left hand he holds a text containing the essence of all that can be taught.

Because the absolute and relative truths are inseparable in his being,

He holds his two hands crossed at his heart.

He sits amid a mass of rainbow lights which emanate from his pores

And fill the whole of space with the infinite ocean of sutra and tantra.

He is seated on a cinnabar throne supported by four blue and four white lions.

His consort on his left is the dark green of complete accomplishment.

She holds a lotus of ever expanding compassion in her left hand,

While with her right she makes the mudra that brings fearlessness to all.

3

The Dharma Lord Manjusrikirti-Yasas

Sits like the gold noon sun

On a golden throne before a wish-fulfilling tree.

His skin is the color of sunrise, and his eyes are blue and piercing.

His expression is fresh and completely alert.

His blue-black mustache and hair are elegantly arranged.

He wears the gold brocade turban and gold crown of a dharma king

Surmounted by a blue diamond bright as the sky just before dawn.

He wears an outer turquoise robe embroidered with golden dragons.

His under robe is made from spun gold.

His sash is red as the first light on a mountain range.

He wears the gold necklaces, earrings and bracelets of an earth-protector.

In his right hand, he holds the stem of a lotus as broad as the sky.

On this rests the flaming vajra sword which, instantaneously

And without moving, cuts through the darkness of ignorance.

Because the treasury of true wisdom is never lost,

In his left hand, he holds aloft a text.

Encountering him, one is suddenly overcome with happiness,

As if one had never known uncertainty or self-doubt.

4

During this great Dharma Rajah's reign in Shambhala,

Many of his subjects in each of the four castes

Followed paths other than the Buddha's way.

Their disputes grew and provoked uncertainty throughout the kingdom.

The great lord then proclaimed his intention

Based on the teachings of Kalacakra

To unite all secular and spiritual paths inseparably

In the single and unchanging ground of basic goodness.

Thus he proclaimed all to be members of the single Vajra caste.

145

Those Brahmins who did not follow the Buddha's way were distressed.

They could not bear to abandon the deities of their ancestors.

They met and decided they had no choice but to leave for India,

So in a great caravan they passed through the ice mountain walls surrounding Shambhala

And began to make their way south.

But Manjusrikirti Yaksas saw Shambhala would be weakened

If the ancient Indian gods, Brahma, Vishnu, Shiva, Rama, and the rest

As well as those who sacrificed to them

Could not find a place within his Dharma and his realm.

Thus, while sitting on his throne in Kalapa,

Manjusrikirti Yasas appeared before them on the road,

And all the worshippers of the ancient gods felt transported to Kalapa.

Suddenly they found themselves in the great Park of Malaya.

There all saw the inseparable Body, Speech and Mandalas of Glorious Kalachakra.

And they saw the entire panoply of Hindu gods and goddesses

Dancing in attendance on the Lord of Time.

They woke as from a dream and returned to Shambhala

Having no desire for any other path.

The dharma king Manjusri Yasas then perfected and taught

The condensed Kalachakra in five chapters.

Thus he showed the outer sign of the E-VAM

To be inseparable from the realization of the meaning of E-VAM.

This inner E-VAM spontaneously produces outer E-VAM.

It is the absolute union of prajna and upaya,

Kalachakra without caste,

Inseparable from Vajrasattva, and the First Buddha.

(4)

As is said in the Root Tantra:

In the middle of the E syllable,

The absolute luminous realm of space,

Is the VAM syllable,

Vajrasattva.

It receives all the bliss of the Buddhas.

This is kaya of bindu, moon and semen

Established by the union of body, speech and mind.

Within the relative phenomena of E,

The relative reality of menstrual blood, sun and speech
Expresses the darkness of mind.

By the union of body, speech and mind,
Within the unified mandalas of body, speech and mind,
By body, speech, mind and desire themselves,
The pure nature of the three worlds exists.   (5)

This is sealed with the words:
Completely beyond existence and non-existence,
Non-duality wears out things and non-things
Inseparable in emptiness and compassion:
This is the Vajra Yoga, the Great Bliss.

Beyond the nature of any ultimate dharmas,
Empty dharmas are completely abandoned,
Free from eternalism and nihilism:
This is the Vajra Yoga without a caste.   (6)

And so it is said:
With inseparable prajna and upaya,
It is non-dual wisdom.
It has no families and no bias.

It transcends the changeable bliss of the world's desirable qualities.

It transcends the dharmas of consciousness.   (7)

And finally:

This indestructible vajra yoga

Is the changeless bliss of Kalachakra,

The first Buddha without a last;

The first Buddha without a caste;

The vajra good fortune of all;

The union of the variety of all;

The meaning of the 12 aspects of truth;

The holder of the 16 aspects of suchness.   (8)

Thus this great lord became the first in the line of **Rigden Kings.**

The first in the line of "Those Who Hold the Caste',

The first in a line that shines like sunlight

Through the shifting clouds of time.

Thus in the ever changing human realm

He establishes limitless and signless ground,

The beginningless and endless expanse.

This is the totality of all phenomena: the cosmic mirror.

Thus Manjusrikirti Yasas proclaimed nowness

As the Svabhavikakaya, the complete body of all the Buddhas.

RIGDEN PUNDARIKA

1

The second Rigden of Shambhala, Pundarika,

The White Lotus, Cherished by Avalokiteshvara,

Now emerges within the Crystal Pavilion of the Kalapa Court.

The Rigden Pundarika enters this world

As an emanation of the transcendent Bodhisattva,

Avalokiteshvara, the Lord of Inconceivable Mercy.

This great Bodhisattva stands erect like the axis of the universe.

He has eleven faces and a thousand arms.

Because he has accomplished all the paths and stages,

And because his love of beings radiates throughout the ten directions,

Ten faces rise from the crown of his head.

Three of the faces are peaceful, three are loving,

Three are indomitably fierce.

And because he is the brilliant compassion of all Buddhas,

His topmost face is Amitabha himself.

Like the rays of the moon on a misty night,

His thousand arms radiate in a circle around him.

These are the thousand arms of a thousand universal monarchs.

In the palm of each hand are the thousand eyes of all the Buddhas.

With his three right hands,

Avalokitesvara holds the mala of ceaseless intention;

He holds the golden eight-spoked wheel of spiritual and temporal law;

And he makes the gesture of limitless offering.

In his three left hands, he holds the white lotus

Which is enlightenment come to full bloom from compassion,

The bow and arrow of meditation and wisdom,

And the vase of immortality which is enlightenment as boundless life.

With two hands in angeli at his heart, he holds the wish-fulfilling jewel,

The inseparability of wisdom and love.

Thus he is the heart of the mind,

Present and immediate in all realms and all times.

2

Before a mass of soft white clouds,

The Rigden Pundarika sits in the clear white light of early dawn,

On the gold eight-lion throne of Shambhala.

He is very youthful and his skin is white as the morning star.

His eyes are dark and he looks on the world with a tender smile.

He wears the gold crown of a dharma king

At the tip of which is set a white opal which radiates light

In the patterns and colors of all the realms.

His robe is the pale orange of first light embroidered with
sleeping tigers.

His sash is the dark blue of cloudless winter sky.

He wears the gold necklaces, earrings, and bracelets of an earth-
protector.

Because every atom of his being and all his actions,

Flow from the warmth of unconditional love,

His hands are crossed at his heart

And in each he holds the green stem of a living white lotus;

Each blossoms like the clouds in a morning sky.

Seeing him, one feels free from every kind of concern or pain,

And so it is like something known only in a moment or a dream.

3

In his unchanging inner form, the Rigden Pundarika

Is pale as moonlight and his expression is gentle and at ease.

In the top-knot of his black hair is the Buddha himself.

Because he is the master of all mediations of form,

He wears a gold meditation belt on his right shoulder.

Because he is the master of meditations not reliant on form,

He wears the skin of a blue antelope over his left shoulder.

In his right hand, he holds a mala made of pearls,

And in his left, a pink lotus in full bloom unfolding through time.

Naked to the waist, he wears a red skirt embroidered with swirling clouds

And orange pants embroidered with countless golden suns.

He sits on a circular golden throne,

And his feet rest on moon disks which float on a crimson lotus.

On his left, his golden consort holds her hands in angeli.

Because every movement of his mind is unconditioned love,

Because every thought that rises spontaneously in his mind

Is the innate freedom of every sentient being,

He is the golden ocean of unconditional fearlessness,

He is the Mahasukhakhaya, the form of bliss of all the Buddhas.

He is the Great Eastern Sun.

4

The Rigden Pundarika, seeing the needs of beings

And the shape of time,

Composed the commentary on the Kalachakra,

The Vimalaprabha, the stainless all-pervasive light of Kalachakra
himself.

In this form, they spread to the rest of the human realm

And so remain.

*

THE BRILLIANT SUCCESSION OF THE LORDS OF KALAPA

II.4.10

RIGDEN BHADRA

1

Now, the third Rigden of Shambhala, Bhadra,

The Good Auspicious One, He Who Rules With The Thousand-
Spoked Wheel,

Entered the Crystal Pavilion of the Kalapa Court and assumes the
throne.

He is the emanation of Yamantaka, Lord of Death.

2

As sunlight touches the peaks of the cold mountains behind him,

The Rigden Bhadra sits on the gold eight-lion throne of Shambhala.

His skin glistens with the color of new snow in first light.

His eyes shine like water at the bottom of a deep well,

And his gaze rests deep within even as he looks out.

His blue-black hair, mustache and small beard are long.

He wears the gold brocade turban and gold crown of a dharma king

Surmounted by a sapphire moonstone

Radiating a still and all-pervasive glow.

His outer robe is pure white as a cumulus cloud and embroidered in silver with standing lions.

His under-robe is made from spun silver.

His sash is the color of saffron.

He wears the gold necklaces, earrings and bracelets of an earth-protector.

Because his mind is like the sky and does not alter

Regardless of season or display,

He holds in his right hand the golden eight-spoked wheel of changeless reality,

In his left hand, he holds the conch

Whose sound compels all movement in the three worlds.

Encountering him is like standing alone in a high mountain forest

Before a deep and silent turquoise lake.

3

The Rigden Bhadra is the auspiciousness of all the Rigdens.

In his unchanging inner form, he is white as mother of pearl.

His gaze is serene and easy, and his mind rests in motionless flow.

Because all forms of thought are resolved in non-thought,

A gold five-pointed vajra is braided into the black hair of his top-knot.

He wears the jeweled crown of the five Tathaghatas.

He wears the green shawl of complete accomplishment draped over his white shoulders.

He wears necklaces and bracelets of gold and sapphires.

Because wisdom and offering are inseparable,

His right hand makes the mudra of ceaseless teaching

And holds the stem of a white lotus

On which stands a gold and jeweled dharmachakra.

Because he holds all the movements of mind

Which bind and separate the elements as beings and realms,

His left hand is in the mudra of unfabricated meditation,

And a pure white conch rests in his palm.

Naked to the waist, he wears pants of dawn-red silk

Embroidered in gold and silver with the sun and moon

And a lapis blue skirt embroidered with clouds and stars.

He sits on a square gold and coral throne.

His consort on his right is, like him, the color of mother of pearl

And her hands make the mudras of fearlessness and of teaching.

By holding the law of secular and spiritual life inseparable

In the heart of unshakable equanimity,

Without effort or purpose he binds

The Wisdom Dharmakaya of the Buddha himself

And the Kingdom of Shambhala in the secret court of all the
Rigdens.

*

RIGDEN VIJAYA

1

Now, the fourth Rigden of Shambhala, Vijaya,

The Victorious One, He Who Magnetizes Wealth and Is
Victorious In Battle,

Takes his seat in the Crystal Pavilion of the Kalapa Court.

The Rigden Vijaya is the victory of all the Rigdens.

He is the emanation of Kshitigharba.

2

In the center of his court-room suffused with crystal light,

The Rigden Vijaya sits on the gold eight-lion throne of
Shambhala.

He is in the full power of his youth.

His beardless face is bluish and dark.

His eyes are yellow; his expression is stern; and he is impressive

As a mass of snow-clouds hurtling across a mountain range.

He wears the gold brocade turban and gold crown of a dharma
king

Surmounted by a ruby

Which fills the room with a cool pinkish light.

His outer robe is red silk embroidered with attacking garudas.

His inner robe is made from spun platinum.

His sash is white as an egret's plume.

He wears the gold necklaces, earrings and bracelets of an earth-protector.

Because he utterly subdues ignorance, rage, greed, craving, and envy

And returns them to their pure state,

In his right hand in the gesture of destruction,

He holds the gold vajra prod with its blade of meteoric iron.

Because he reaches into the heart of all his subjects

And binds them to the spontaneous presence of wisdom,

In his left hand in the gesture of meditation,

He holds an iron rope with an iron hook and ring.

Encountering him is to feel both empty and full

As if one were lost in a blizzard.

While the world becomes indistinct amid huge soft snow-flakes.

One is both overwhelmed with its beauty and is painfully alone.

In his unchanging inner form, he is absolutely complete.

He is dark verdant green like pine forest.

His expression is gentle and full of peace.

Because every movement of his mind appears as oceans of
galaxies of mandalas,

A golden vajra is braided into his top-knot.

Because the five wisdoms are spontaneously realized,

He wears the crown of the five Tathagathas.

Because he rests in complete simplicity, he is naked to the waist.

Because all that moves within the mind are his ornaments,

He wears necklaces, bracelets and anklets of gold.

In his right hand, he holds the three jewels inseparable,

The Buddha, the Dharma, and the sangha, all ablaze in golden
light.

Because all beings are provided with whatever is needed

To overcome the poverty of ego-fixation,

In his left hand, he holds an immense wish-fulfilling tree in full
bloom.

He wears red pants embroidered with rain-clouds

And a red skirt embroidered with flowers.

He sits on a gold and black cushion on a gold enameled black
lacquer throne

Whose high red back is like a palace.

His snow white consort on his right looks lovingly upon the world,

And with her raised right hand makes the mudra of protecting.

Around them, goddesses make endless offerings of melodious sound.

Because he experiences no distinction between motion and motionless,

Sacred and secular, phenomena and wisdom deity,

Everything is accomplished, and there is nothing that needs completion.

There is no enemy and no impoverishment.

He binds the unceasing Sambhogakaya of the Buddha himself.

Into the Kingdom of Shambhala in the inner court of all the Rigdens.

*

THE BRILLIANT SUCCESSION OF THE LORDS OF KALAPA

II.4.12

RIGDEN SUMITRA

1

Now, the fifth Rigden of Shambhala, Sumitra,

The Good Friend, He Who Unifies Means and Wisdom,

The Victor over Samsara,

Enters the Crystal Pavilion of the Kalapa Court.

2

Amid sprays of budding trees,

The Rigden Sumitra sits at ease on a green silk carpet.

Though in late middle age, he is vigorous.

His face is warm and ruddy

And his mustache, short beard and hair are still the color of
ebony.

His eyes are blue and his expression is affectionate and cheerful.

He exudes indomitable confidence.

He wears the gold crown of a dharma king

Surmounted by a blazing diamond whose light glistens
everywhere.

His robe is blue silk embroidered in gold with hosts of playful
dragons.

His sash is the color of red maple leaves.

He wears the gold necklace and earrings of an earth protector.

He holds in his right hand the black arrow of skillful means

Which penetrates all forms of confusion and deceit.

In his left hand he holds the cinnabar bow of wisdom

Which arises spontaneously in every circumstance.

Encountering him is to find a source of unwavering support.

3

The Rigden Sumitra is the unsparing compassion of all the Rigdens.

He is the emanation of Vajrakilaya.

In his unchanging inner form, he is the color of white quartz.

He is enraged against the hordes of doubts, terrors and ambitious cravings

Which flood the earth and torment all who live here.

Nothing escapes the furious gaze of his three eyes.

Because he is inseparable from the five wisdoms,

He wears the crown of the five Tathagathas.

He sits amid an blaze of red light, bright as the time-ending fire.

Because the mind of non-meditation is unadorned,

He is naked to the waist.

And because he will not rest in destroying the traps where all are caught,

He wears a tiger-skin skirt.

Blue green serpents, the subtle elements of mind

That give birth to all the cycles of time,

Are coiled around his neck, arms, wrists and ankles

He wears a golden necklace in which is set the sea-green jewel

Containing the totality of living consciousness.

In his right hand, he holds aloft a gilded ruby-headed mace,

The power of wisdom that stupefies and destroys all conceptual thought.

In his right hand, he holds an iron rope with an iron ring and hook,

Which hooks and binds all forms of emotional craving.

He sits on a red and gold circular throne

Supported in the air by hundreds of dancing dakinis.

Over the back of the throne is thrown the green robe of complete accomplishment.

Because he will even spring into the realms of death,

Hooked on the right side of the throne is a golden lion's head.

His golden consort, standing on his right,

Makes the mudras of fearlessness and subduing.

Because compassion is the heart of union of means and wisdom,

Because compassion is the dance of freedom,

Because compassion is inseparable from light itself,

Because the radiance of compassion can not be obstructed, deflected, or dimmed,

He binds the all-pervading Nirmanakaya of the Buddha himself

To the Kingdom of Shambhala in the outer court of all the Rigdens.

*

THE BRILLIANT SUCCESSION OF THE LORDS OF KALAPA

II.4.13

RIGDEN RAKTAPANI

1

Now, the sixth Rigden of Shambhala, Raktapani,

He Whose Hand Is Red, touching with the essence of life,

Holder of the Blissful Vajra and Bell,

Takes his seat in the Crystal Pavilion of the Kalapa Court.

2

On the cinnabar porch of his throne room.

The Rigden Raktapani sits on the gold eight-lion throne of Shambhala.

His skin is dark gold and his broad impassive face is unlined and ageless.

His eyes are obsidian black and glitter as if with the light beneath the surface of a deep lake.

His black hair and mustache are fine and smooth.

He wears the gold crown of a dharma king

In whose apex is set a dark blue glowing sapphire.

His outer robe is deep orange embroidered with dancing tiger cubs.

His inner robe is made of spun gold.

His silk sash is bluish purple.

He wears the gold necklace and earrings of an earth protector.

In his right hand, he holds the stem of a vast white lotus

On whose red anthers rest a golden five-pointed vajra

Blazing with the light of a ceaseless dawn.

In his left hand, he holds at his waist a silver ghanta,

Bell upward as a cup containing all the sounds and movements of the world.

He sits absolutely motionless, and encountering him

Is like being struck by a lightning bolt.

3

The Rigden Raktapani is the all-pervasive simplicity of all the
Rigdens .

In his unchanging inner form,

He is deep blue like the sky before time moved.

He is youthful and at ease, and his face is unwavering and still.

Because the vastness of his mind cannot be penetrated,

He wears a gold five-pointed vajra braided in his top-knot.

Because he experiences all the passions as vivid and unborn,

He wears the gold crown of the five Tathaghatas.

Because he is indestructible light,

A diamond hangs on a gold chain at his heart.

Because the births and deaths innumerable of beings

Move unfettered within his changeless being,

He wears necklaces, bracelets and anklets of gold.

Because time is complete accomplishment,

He wears a billowing green silk scarf.

In his right hand, he holds a golden vajra ax with a blade of
meteoric iron.

Which severs the brilliance of the ayatanas from the limits of
origin.

In the vast space of his unmoving mind,

Klesha and samskara are the pattern of the universe,

Are cut from clinging to the fear of death or hope of continuing.

So in his left hand, he holds three freshly severed heads.

He wears rainbow-colored pants and a red skirt

Embroidered in gold and silver with galaxies of suns and moons.

He sits on a square red and black gilded throne

Supported by eight white snow-lions.

Because he is the lord of the three worlds,

The throne has a three-tiered back and is surmounted by the three jewels.

His consort is seated on his right, shining deep blue like a timeless sky.

Because the indestructible mind and the totality of phenomena

Are completely inseparable in bliss,

She holds a gold five-pointed vajra aloft in her right hand

And a silver bell upwards at her heart.

Because he is the mind that does not know beginning or end,

He is nowness.

He is the vastness of the ayatanas,

And thus he binds the thought lineage of the Victorious Ones

To the thought lineage of the Rigden Kings

*

THE BRILLIANT SUCCESSION OF THE LORDS OF KALAPA

II.4.14

RIGDEN VISNUGUPTA

1

Now, the seventh **Rigden of Shambhala, Visnugupta,**

The Secret of Visnu, The Smiling Holder of Trident and Rosary,

Enters into the Crystal Pavilion of the Kalapa Court.

2

In his throne room adorned with red and white peonies,

The Rigden Visnugupta sits erect on the gold eight-lion throne.

He is vibrant and youthful. His face is the color of a spring moon.

His eyes are deep blue and his expression is at ease but passionate.

The radiance of his effortless awareness is all-pervasive.

He wears the gold crown of a dharma king

Surmounted by a glowing ruby.

His outer robe is white silk embroidered with gold hunting lions.

His inner robe is made from spun gold.

His sash is shiny and the color of saffron.

He wears the gold necklace and earrings of an earth protector.

In his right hand, he holds a gold trident on an ebony pole

Adorned with a lion's mane and a yellow banner.

The trident's three points are past, present and future.

They are the three root actions: creating, preserving and destroying.

They are the three nadis.

The trident is the blazing weapon of nowness,

Penetrating passion, ignorance and aggression.

In his left hand, he holds a crystal rosary

Each of whose beads reflects the brilliance of the ayatanas.

Encountering him is like becoming dizzy

From the subtle scent of an unknown perfume.

3

The Rigden Visnugupta is the endless being of all the Rigdens.

And in his unchanging inner form,

He is deep cobalt blue, like evening in late spring.

He is youthful and vibrant, and he gazes ardently into fathomless space.

Because he is spontaneously present in all lights and colors,

He wears the crown of the Five Tathagathas adorned with five colored jewels.

Because he is alive in the solid and in the insubstantial,

He wears necklaces, bracelets and anklets of gold.

Because he shines in all movement, he wears a swirling green scarf.

As the essence of the display of boundless space,

In his right hand, he shows a golden fiv- pointed vajra.

And because the primordial utterance of space is ever present,

He holds a text at the level of his heart.

He wears orange silk pants embroidered with golden stars,

And because he appears even in the veil of conflicting emotions,

He wears a red translucent shawl.

He sits on a square red and black gilt throne with an emerald seat,

And his left foot rests on the tree whose trunk is the axis of the universe.

His consort stands beside him on his left,

Dark green, and adorned with a coral-colored shawl,

She holds the golden thread of innate continuity.

Because he is the primordial voice from which all phenomena take shape,

He is spontaneous freedom and insatiable passion;

Thus he binds the sign lineage of the Vidyadharas

To the sign lineage of the Rigden Kings.

*

THE BRILLIANT SUCCESSION OF THE LODS OF KALAPA

II.4.15

RIGDEN ARKAKIRTI
1

Now, the eighth Rigden of Shambhala, Arkakirti,

Friend of the Radiant Sun, The Annihilator of Wild Demons,

Takes his place in the Crystal Pavilion of the Kalapa Court.

He is the emanation of Bodhisattva Akashagharba.

2

In the center of his throne room, amid roar of a gathering gale,

The Rigden Arkakirti sits on the gold eight-lion throne of Shambhala.

He is youthful and his skin is very dark.

His eyes are black and bulging and his expression is fierce.

His heavy dark eyebrows are like thunder clouds.

His mind is without fear or limit, and his appetites are urgent and unbridled.

He wears the gold crown of a dharma king

In whose apex is set an emerald

Which fills the room with the green glow which precedes a thunderstorm.

His outer robe is crimson embroidered with silver garudas,

And his inner robe is made of spun silver.

His silk sash is creamy white.

He wears the necklace and earrings of an earth protector.

In his right hand he holds a hooked knife with a blade of meteoric iron

Which cuts through the survival mind and opens the brilliance of relative truth.

Because all the phenomena of body and mind are the turbulent expanse of radiant bliss,

In his left hand, he holds a kapala filled with a golden ocean of amrita.

Encountering him, one is terrified

As if one's life were to be stolen away.

The Rigden Arkakirti is the vivid, all-pervasive teaching of all the Rigdens.

In his unchanging secret form, he is bright blue like a cornflower.

He is youthful, vibrant and very much at ease.

His expression is one-pointed and intent.

Because his mind rests in simplicity, his top-knot is unadorned.

Because he enters in to the play of the senses completely and is completely pure,

His crown and necklace are garlands of red and white lotuses, fragrant and fresh.

He is the spontaneous presence of wisdom,

Thus he wears gold necklaces, earrings and anklets encrusted with jewels.

Because he reaches out to all who encounter him,

The green shawl of complete accomplishment billows around him.

In his right hand, he holds the stem of a vast white lotus

On which stands the blazing sword of the unmistaken view.

In his left hand, he holds the stem of an immense red lotus

On which stands a crimson source of dharmas,

The origin of all phenomena and of all times.

Thus he has realized the non-duality of life and awareness.

Because realization and action are inseparable in his being,

His hands are crossed at the level of his heart.

And because he will guide every being to freedom in the natural state,

His right hand is held in the teaching mudra.

He wears rainbow-colored pants and a skirt of plain red silk.

On his square red and gold enameled throne,

He is seated on a silver moon disc resting on the green anthers

Of a white lotus as vast as the universe.

His golden consort seated on his right

Holds a skull cup of deathless amrita and a world-creating white conch.

Together, they sit amid a whirling mass of rainbow light

As all the many forms of light that shine in space

Join in a single place, and leave no room for doubt or fear.

Arising from the inseparability of body, speech, mind, quality and action,

Which is the complete expression of unfabricated reality,

Showing this path, which is life itself,

He binds the oral lineage of the living guru.

To the oral lineage of the Rigden King.

*

THE BRILLIANT SUCCESSION OF THE LORDS OF KALAPA

II.4.16

RIGDEN SUBHADRA

1

Now, the ninth Rigden of Shambhala, Subhadra,

Great Auspiciousness, Holder of the Sword and Shield,

Rules in the Crystal Pavilion of the Kalapa Court.

He is the emanation of the first Lord of Dralas.

2

In the morning sunlight of his gold and cinnabar throne room,

The Rigden Subhadra sits on the gold eight-lion throne of Shambhala

With his right leg under him and his left leg on the ground

As if he were about to leap up suddenly.

His face is bright and shiny as new gold,

And his green eyes glitter with eagerness.

He is very still and his powerful body is perfectly controlled.

His beard, mustache and long black hair are immaculate.

He wears the gold crown of a dharma king

Surmounted by a clear crystal, bright from within like a morning sky.

His robe is pale turquoise blue, embroidered with diving silver dragons.

He wears a dark blue pleated cape embroidered with his imperial seals.

His sash is red as fresh blood.

In his right hand, he holds a vajra-handled flaming sword

Whose double blades cut the net of cause and effect

Returning all outer and inner phenomena to empty space.

Because nowness is complete self-existing protection,

In his left hand, he holds a golden shield adorned with a tiger's mane

And marked with a coil of joy resting on a lotus.

Meeting him is like seeing a dragon flying easily in the sky.

He can be neither propitiated nor appeased.

3

The Rigden Subhadra is the success of all the Rigdens.

In his inner form, he is immense and blue-black, absorbing all light

As if there were a hole in the universe.

His is terrifying, utterly enraged. His three eyes blaze like knives,

And his teeth gleam like diamond daggers.

His eyebrows, mustache and beard are burning

Red like forest fires advancing on a mountain slope.

He is the zero point between existence and non-existence.

Because he is the completely indestructible state,

His wears a gold five-pointed vajra at the tip of his blazing red top-knot.

Locks of his hair cascade down his shoulders like lava from a volcano.

Because all manifestations of wisdom are reduced in him to a single point,

He wears a gold crown adorned with five dried skulls.

Because the myriad cycles of creation are merely momentary ornaments,

He wears blue-green serpents as necklaces, bracelets and anklets.

Because all thoughts of permanent happiness are illusions,

He wears gold necklaces and arm-bands.

Because he completely flays apart all false views,

He wears a fresh snow-lion skin around his shoulders.

He wears the skin of a she-tiger around his waist.

All passions, stripped from karma adorn him.

A dark green shawl swirls around his neck

As all possibilities are fulfilled in the immensity of silence.

Because creation and destruction emerge equally from his being,

In his right hand, he holds aloft a five-pointed vajra of pure gold

Emitting hailstorms and swirls of lightning.

In his left, he holds an immense blue serpent

Whose hissing is the wind of all winds and the origin of life.

He sits with his right leg extended on a gold and crimson enameled throne

Which is supported by a host of animal-headed female demons

Who scream and screech with terrifying fury.

Because this is the quintessence of the three refuges and the three roots,

At the summit of the throne back, the three jewels blaze unceasingly.

His consort, naked and smoky black,

Wearing a crown of skulls and a serpent necklace,

Sits at his left and holds a gold eight-spoked wheel of the true law,

And a gold vase containing the elixir that pervades life and death.

He is timelessness itself, beyond the constraints of birth and death.

He is end, origin and continuity, the all-consuming naked face of truth.

Therefore he binds the lineage of indivisible, indestructible reality

To the Absolute Ashe of the Rigden Kings.

THE BRILLIANT SUCCESSION OF THE LORDS OF KALAPA

II.4.17

RIGDEN SAMUDRAVIJAYA

1

Now, the tenth Rigden of Shambhala, Samudravijaya,

The Ocean of Victory, the Annihilator of All Demons,

Occupies the Crystal Hall of the Kalapa Court.

He is the emanation of Vajrapani.

2

In a high mountain valley alive with new grass beneath a sky of
massing rain clouds,

The Rigden Samudravijaya sits poised on the high eight-lion
throne of Shambhala.

He is youthful but with the full strength of manhood.

His smooth amber-colored face has an intense reddish glow.

His eyes are black, deep and penetrating.

And his black hair is smooth and oiled.

He wears the gold crown of a dharma king

Surmounted with an orb of gzhi marked with a black Ashe

Which vibrates and pulses and makes the air heavy.

His outer robe is pink-orange like a sunrise, embroidered with stalking tigers.

His inner robe is deep black silk.

His silk sash is the color of turquoise.

He wears the gold earring and necklace of an earth protector.

He cannot be deceived.

He will not permit the hearts of his people to be drawn down into degradation.

So in his right hand he holds a gold vajra ax with a blade of meteoric iron.

When it flashes through the air in a brilliant arc of light,

The stroke of his blade rouses primordial confidence,

And expands the domain of enlightened society in the heart of the human realm.

In his left hand, he holds by the hair, the severed head of the walking corpse of egotism.

He sits with his left leg extended, as if ready to stride off his throne.

Encountering him, one is intimidated and jealous.

One longs to know him.

3

The Rigden Samudravijaya is the victory stroke of all the Rigdens.

In his unchanging inner form, he is red and vibrant.

His body is itself a blazing fire of love and compassion, consuming every fear.

He is youthful, sits upright and is very still.

His face is gentle and his gaze encompasses

The ever-changing dance of life.

Because his mind is a stainless mirror,

He wears a blazing sapphire at the summit of his top-knot.

Because his mind indestructible,

A gold five-pointed vajra is braided in his hair below it.

He wears a gold crown of emeralds and rubies set on budding lotuses

Since he is completely immersed in all passions and actions

That emerge and radiate in the boundless ayatanas.

Because wisdom and complete accomplishment are inseparable

in experience,

He wears gold necklaces, anklets and bracelets adorned with glittering sapphires and emeralds.

Because he cherishes the poignant and beautiful pulse of life,

Expanding and contracting without end,

He wears a garland of red and white lotuses in full bloom.

Because enlightened activity is all-pervasive,

He wears a green and blue silk shawl.

In the non-dual ground of unconditional compassion and innate purity,

All the moments of life and death are the timeless radiance of victory.

So, in his right hand, he holds the stem of a vast red lotus in full bloom

On which stand the jewels blazing in a mass of gold light.

So in his left hand, he holds the stem of a vast white lotus in full bloom

On which stands a gold vase of deathless amrita.

His communication is unceasing and everywhere,

Therefore with both hands he makes the mudra of teaching.

He wears a shimmering red silk skirt embroidered with flames,

And sits on a square gold and cinnabar throne whose back is like a storm cloud.

Because the reality of enlightened society is achieved instantly,

His consort, blue like a summer night, seated at his left,

Holds out a golden bowl bearing many perfect kinds of fruit.

Present in every heartbeat,

Expanding in every longing,

Bright in every thought,

Alive in every sight, smell, taste, touch and sound

This is the blessing of the spontaneous lineage of all-pervasive awareness,

The living Black Ashe of the Rigden King.

*

THE BRILLIANT SUCCESSION OF THE LORDS OF KALAPA

II.4.17

RIGDEN AJA

1

Now, the eleventh Rigden of Shambhala, Aja,

The Unborn and Invincible He Who Binds With Unbreakable Iron Chains,

Dwells in the Crystal Pavilion of the Kalapa Court.

He is the emanation of Yamantaka.

2

Beneath a vast cedar tree in the white jade courtyard of his palace,

The Rigden Aja sits on a white and gold embroidered throne.

He is very youthful and his face is pale white like moonlight on quartz.

His eyes are the color of gray crystal.

In the light of his unmoving gaze,

The union of the fathomless depth of primordial awareness

And the vast expanse of empty space are complete.

Though his expression is grave, he smiles softly.

His fine black hair is combed back.

He wears the gold crown of a dharma king

At whose apex is diamond clear as water.

His outer robe is lustrous pure white silk,

And his inner robe is spun silver.

His brocade silk sash is pale gold, the color just before sunrise.

He wears the gold necklace and earrings of an earth protector.

In his right hand, he holds a meteoric iron mace

Which effortlessly crushes all the illusory solidity of conceptual thought,

And in his left hand, he holds an adamantine iron chain

That effortlessly binds all the torrential winds of conflicting emotion.

So without stirring, without the slightest movement of his mind,

185

By the pure luminosity of rigpa itself,

All apparent delusions resolve in the empty expanse of primordial space.

To encounter him is like standing on a broad empty plain beneath a cloudless sky.

Hollow terror and brilliant vividness are joined inextricably.

3

The Rigden Aja is the invincible radiance of all the Rigdens.

In his unchanging inner form, he is immense and white as a chalk cliff.

His expression is full of rage and fury. He cannot be appeased.

His three blood-shot eyes see everything and his gaze cannot be evaded.

With fangs like a jagged snow-mountain range, he bites his red lower lip.

His gold beard, eyebrows and hair swirl with a roaring sound

Like an immense palace exploding on fire.

Because he conquers everything, he wears the gold crown of the five Tathaghatas.

Because illusions of origin and attainment, past and future,

Fill the whole of space,

He wears gold necklaces with rubies and sapphires,

Gold anklets and earrings;

He wears a writhing black serpent around his neck

Whose tail and head are twined at the level of his secret center.

Green serpents hang on his wrists and black ones on his ankles.

Because passion and destruction are inseparable,

A scarf, red on the inside, green on the outside, swirls from his neck.

He is naked except for a tiger-skin round his waist.

In his raised right hand, he brandishes the flaming vajra sword,

Eternally and instantly severing the unchanging from the changing,

The pure from the impure.

In his left hand at his heart, he holds the unbreakable cord with a golden hook and ring at either end.

Eternally and inseparably binding the changing and unchanging,

The impure and pure.

He is surrounded by a towering mass of roaring flames

Consuming all the intricate fabric of time.

His throne is a square chariot, red, black, and gold, vast as half the earth.

It trundles across the sky on eight-spoked wheels like a roaring flood.

It is pulled by five snow-lions, three white with black manes,

Two turquoise with red manes who gambol and prance,

Drawing the cart that crushes all beneath it.

His consort seated on his right is smoky black,

Naked but for a tiger-skin around her waist.

Her face is enraged, and she holds out a gold hooked knife and a skull cup,

Showing the inseparability of radiant bliss and luminous non-thought.

This is the sovereign mind of mirror-like wisdom,

The invincible and unborn vision of the Great Eastern Sun

In the timeless mind of the Rigden Kings.

*

THE BRILLIANT SUCCESSION OF THE LORDS OF KALAPA

II.4.19

RIGDEN SURYA

1

Now, the twelfth Rigden of Shambhala, Surya,

The Sun, The All-Pervading Radiant Jewel Light,

Appears in the Crystal Pavilion of the Kalapa Court.

He is the emanation of Bodhisattva Kshitigharba.

2

On the crystal roof of his golden palace beneath a sky full of towering white clouds,

The Rigden Surya sits on a heap of golden cushions

On the gold eight-lion throne of Shambhala.

He is full of the vigor of early manhood.

His skin is bright gold and smooth and his expression is watchful and reflective.

His features are broad and his lips red and moist.

His pale blue eyes are peaceful and without moving take in everything.

His blue-black hair is oiled and bound in a top-knot.

He wears the gold crown of a dharma king,

Surmounted by a blue diamond whose light is like an empty sky.

His outer robe is bright orange embroidered with gold prowling tigers.

His inner robe is the color of kingfisher feathers.

His silk sash is the color of a blue iris.

He wears the gold necklace and earrings of an earth protector.

With his raised right hand, he plays a hand drum made from male and female human skulls.

As he plays, the drumheads resonate together.

In the pulse of their resonance, all concepts arise, make shapes, dissolve.

In his left hand, at the level of his secret center,

He holds the origin of all display,

Jewels of five colors that vibrate amid a mass of gold flames.

His simplicity is daunting.

Encountering him, one feels oneself dissolving

In an ocean of motionless clarity.

3

The Rigden Surya is the radiant peace of all the Rigdens.

In his unchanging inner form, he is a bright and fathomless dark blue,

Like the horizon of night on a fragrant and quiet late spring evening.

He is youthful and at ease, and his two eyes glow like crescent moons.

Because all the enticements of the senses and all the movements of the passions

Are known precisely and resolved in his mirror-like mind,

He wears a garland of pink lotuses, a gold crown adorned with rubies and sapphires.

Because all phenomena are accommodated in the boundless peace of great compassion,

His top-knot is bound only with a simple red silk cord.

Sparkling gold necklaces, bracelets, earrings and anklets

Adorn his dark body like galaxies of stars.

Because he overcomes all forms of arrogance, fear and small-mindedness,

He wears a billowing shawl, pale blue on the inside, shimmering white on the outside.

He is surrounded by vermilion light, embracing the three worlds.

In his right hand, he holds the stem of a red lotus in full bloom,

The living form of compassion,

On which stand a blazing sapphire vajra sword of prajna.

Then because the spontaneous wisdom penetrating all discursive thought

Is inseparable from the gates of the ayatanas,

In the same hand, he also holds an emerald arrow

Attached to whose tip is a gold chain twined with flowers.

In his left hand, he holds the stem of the vast white lotus

On which rests the complete text of the dharma,

And he also holds a white ivory bow,

This because the primordial purity of all phenomena is the only support

For the lineage of transmitted wisdom and for its practice.

He wears rainbow-colored pants and a red silk skirt,

And sits directly and indifferently on the squirming red body of raga, continuous craving

And the thrashing white body of kroda, endless rage.

His square throne in made of gold and bronze.

To his right sits his consort, blue as a deep lake beneath a dawn sky.

She holds, in her right hand on her hip, a hooked knife

And in her left, at her heart, she holds a skull cup of blissful amrita.

Together they are surrounded by the all-pervasive light

Of the ever-rising sun.

He is beyond all complexity and his limitless mind

Spontaneously pacifies all the delusions of fear.

Thus he binds mirror-like wisdom

To the Tiger vision of the Rigden Kings.

*

RIGDEN VISVARUPA

1

Now, the thirteenth Rigden of Shambhala, Visvarupa,

He Whose Body is the Universe of Forms, He Who Holds the Vajra Goad and Noose,

Rules in the Crystal Palace of the Kalapa Court.

He is the emanation of Vajrakilaya.

2

Sitting on a wide cinnabar balustrade built on a mountainside

And overlooking the ocean-like expanse of verdant plains,

The Rigden Visvarupa sits on the gold eight-lion throne of Shambhala.

He is mature and powerful, and his skin is dark gold and glowing.

As he surveys his kingdom with gold-flecked black eyes,

His expression is alert and fierce.

His black mustache is clipped and his hair combed back.

He wears the gold crown of a dharma king

Surmounted by a jeweled top-knot in whose crest an emerald glows

And fills the air with the green light of an approaching storm.

His outer robe of creamy silk, embroidered in gold with mating lions.

His inner silk robe is emerald colored.

His silk sash is the color of a tiger lily.

Because he subjugates all enemies without effort,

In his right hand resting on his knee, he holds a golden vajra prod.

Because he binds everything in the three times to complete fulfillment,

He holds in his left hand a golden noose.

His power has no gaps, and encountering him,

One feels that one is standing on the edge of a cliff in a gale.

3

The Rigden Visvarupa is the activity of all the Rigdens.

In his unchanging inner form, he is bright red and shiny like a glowing ember.

He is youthful, vibrant, and his two eyes light on everything in the world of form.

And because all the secrets of the world beyond form are known and brought to fruition,

He wears a gold crown adorned with sapphires and emeralds.

Because the poverty of ego-fixation is spontaneously destroyed,

His top-knot is bound with a single gold cord.

Gold necklaces, bracelets and anklets sparkle on his red naked body

Like a shower of sparks rising in a fire.

Because all the realms and beings of life and death,

Arising from sleep, dream, and unconsciousness,

Are completely manifested and equivalent in luminosity,

He wears a great black snake poised to strike around his neck,

And smaller snakes around his arms and ankles.

Because all such phenomena are the great bliss,

He wears a garland of red and white lotuses.

In his raised right hand, he holds a golden vajra goad,

Since he has complete power over all the appearances in waking life and dream.

And because the radiance of the ayatanas are fulfilled in time,

He holds a circle of red lotuses in full bloom.

He is completely naked except for a tiger skin around his waist.

His square throne is made of gold, cinnabar and sapphire

With a high red and black cloud back surmounted by a blazing jewel of dharma.

He rides in a great chariot flying through space on four huge wheels of gold

Which grind down all appearances into luminous rays of light.

It is pulled by seven huge steeds of self-existing wind-horse:

Two are the color of lapis,

One the color of turquoise, two the color of conch,

One the color of bronze, and one the color of gold.

His consort seated on his right is pearly white

Makes the mudra of the wheel of law and holds a sapphire begging bowl

Because giving and receiving are one in innate purity.

He experiences the whole of phenomena as unobstructed.

He is beyond any sense of bodily or mental need.

Thus he binds all accomplishing wisdom

With the Lion vision of the Rigden Kings.

*

THE BRILLIANT SUCCESSION OF THE LORDS OF KALAPA

II.4.21

RIGDEN SASIPRABHA

1

Now, the fourteenth **Rigden, Sasiprabha,**

Light of the Moon, the Lord of Secret Mantra and Holder of the Wheel and Conch,

Enters the Crystal Pavilion of the Kalapa Court.

He is the emanation of Sarvanivaranaviskrambin.

2

In the cinnabar throne room of the Kalapa court, amid the rich perfumes of flowers and incense,

The Rigden Sasiprabha sits on the gold eight-lion throne of Shambhala.

He is in the prime of manhood and his still strong passions are controlled.

His skin is the color of red gold, and his expression is passionate and motionless.

His gold eyes shine with eager interest.

His dark lips are slightly parted and his white teeth gleam.

His black mustache and hair are smooth and shiny.

He wears the gold crown of a dharma king,

On whose top a red diamond shines filling the room with ruby light.

His outer robe is vermilion silk, embroidered with gold Garudas, wings outstretched.

His inner robe is heavy crimson satin.

His silk sash is orange like a glowing ember.

He wears the gold necklace and earrings of an earth protector.

In his raised right hand, he holds the gold eight-spoked wheel of law

Which embodies all true instruction on what is to be cultivated and avoided.

In his left hand at his waist, he holds a luminous white conch

From whose subtle turnings all phenomena evolve from emptiness,

And in whose revolutions everything dissolves.

The directness of his love is shocking.

Encountering him is like walking into a room on fire.

The Rigden Sasiprabha is the all-pervasive love of all the
Rigdens.

In his unchanging inner form, he is pure white

And radiant as a full moon in a summer sky.

He is very youthful and at ease.

All is embraced impartially in his loving gaze.

Because he pervades all the outer realms of cause and effect

And all the inner realms of consciousnessness,

He wears a gold crown adorned with sapphires and emeralds

And a deep blue diamond surmounts his top-knot.

Because he is the ground of all the senses,

He wears gold and jeweled necklaces, bracelets and earrings.

Because his love radiates in utter darkness,

He wears a shawl, black on the outside, red on the inside.

Because pure sound is the unchanging essence of binding and
separating,

In all the realms of birth and death,

In his right hand at his heart, he holds a gold and ruby treasure
vase

Which overflows with the amrita of all the vowels and
consonants.

In his left hand, he holds the green stem of a vast pink lotus

On which rests a moon, full beyond waxing and waning,

Unalterable beyond articulation of any kind,

The eternal, clear and peaceful light of the innate.

He wears red silk pants and a red skirt adorned with gold and silver suns and moons.

He gilded square throne is made of cinnabar and lapis.

Sapphires blaze at the sides of its cloud back.

A yogin in the garb of a king and a yogini, white and naked to the waist,

Uphold his throne.

A turquoise lion with an emerald mane prances between them.

Seated on his right is his consort, white as a swan.

She offers a long skein of white silk, the stainless continuity.

All passions and concepts which unite and separate,

Create and destroy the ceaseless panoramas of life

Are inseparable from his immovable love.

Thus he binds discriminating wisdom

To the Garuda vision of the Rigden Kings.

*

THE BRILLIANT SUCCESSION OF THE LORDS OF KALAPA

II.4.22

RIGDEN ANANTA

1

Now the fifteenth Rigden of Shambhala, Ananta,

The Infinite, The Holder of the Hammer Which Breaks Absorption

And The Lotus Of Limitless Compassion,

Enters in the Crystal Palace of the Kalapa Court.

2

On the topmost peak of a snow mountain range amid gold summer clouds,

The Rigden Ananta sits on the gold eight-lion throne of Shambhala.

He is very youthful and his broad face is smooth and hard like polished white jade.

His eyes are deep gold and stare fixedly ahead of him.

His expression is proud and commanding.

His body is slender and lithe,

And his left leg with its iron-soled boot is casually extended.

His black hair is thick and smooth.

He wears the gold crown of a dharma king

Surmounted by a saffron yellow diamond which emits lightning-like flashes.

His outer robe is dark blue silk embroidered in gold with furious dragons.

His inner robe is made of small gold plates.

His silk sash is red, the color of fresh blood.

He wears the gold necklace and earrings of an earth protector.

In his right hand at his waist, he holds the gold vajra hammer

Which crushes all the poverty of ego-fixation.

In his left hand, he holds the green stem of an immense white lotus

Which is the vast primordial space of pure compassion.

His presence is paralyzing.

Encountering him is like suddenly discovering a golden serpent

Alive beneath the covers of one's bed.

3

The Rigden Ananta is the limitlessness of all the Rigdens.

In his unchanging inner form, he is pulsing black, like a dot of ink spreading in an empty sky.

He is completely fearless and his three blood-shot eyes flash like lightening,

Destroying all limits caused by believing in the reality of time.

Because he has exhausted all the impulses of neediness,

He wears a gold crown with five dried skulls.

Because he is the full display of naked mind itself,

His top-knot is completely unadorned.

Because complete compassion is inseparable from the existence of the world of form,

All around his head is a halo of seething hot red light.

Because immersion in the terrors of life and death only expand his fearlessness,

He wears around his shoulders a freshly flayed human skin.

Because without fear, all enjoyment is free from conceptual bias,

He wears a necklace of fifty-two dried human skulls.

Because he gives life freely and continuously,

Writhing green snakes adorn his neck, wrists and ankles.

Because he revels in lust and all that stems from lust,

The great green and white serpent hanging from his neck

Twines its tail and head with flicking tongue at the level of his secret center.

Because he is not afraid to cherish life,

He wears gold and jeweled necklaces, bracelets, arm bands and earrings.

In his right hand he brandishes an iron mace surmounted by a flaming sapphire.

With this he crushes spontaneously all solitary dreams, doubts, and longings,

In the endless and beginningless pulse of life itself.

In his left hand, he holds out a long coil of diamond rope with a hook and noose.

Reaching in through all elaboration or complexity,

He dissolves the limited mind of fear in the infinite ocean of empty bliss.

Because he overwhelms all solidification effortlessly,

He wears the skin of a snow lioness around his waist.

His square throne of gold, cinnabar and bronze is a vast chariot

With four bronze eight-spoked wheels,

Drawn inexorably on by eight night-black ravening sows.

His golden consort, radiant with all desirable qualities,

Stands to his right and offers the mudra of fearlessness

And the wish-fulfilling tree.

They are surrounded by a pulsing mass of rainbow light,

From which everything arises and into which all dissolves.

This is the beginningless beginning and the endless end.

This is the infinity of nowness.

Thus he binds the enriching wisdom of equanimity,

To the Dragon vision of the Rigden Kings.

*

THE BRILLIANT SUCCESSION OF THE LORDS OF KALAPA

II.4.23

RIGDEN MAHIPALA

1

Now, the sixteenth Rigden of Shambhala, Mahipala,

Earth Protector, He Who Holds The Hooked Knife

Which Cuts The Bonds of Ignorance

And The Skull Cup Filled The Amrita of Eternity.

Takes his seat in the Crystal Hall of the Kalapa Court.

He is the emanation of Akashagharba.

2

In the Coral-walled Hall of Justice of the Kalapa Court,

Filled with black vases of red and white peonies,

The Rigden Mahipala sits on the gold eight-lion throne of
Shambhala.

He is in the full bloom of youth and his face is smooth and florid.

His eyes are silver-colored and alert. His features are broad and composed.

His expression is humble yet sure.

His thick body is muscular and strong.

His dark black hair is combed back.

He wears the gold crown of a dharma king,

In whose apex is set a ruby that glows with a pervasive inner light.

He wears a red silk outer robe embroidered in gold with nesting garudas.

His inner robe is made of spun gold.

His silk sash is white as a pearl.

He wears the gold necklace and earrings of an earth protector.

In his right hand at the level of his heart,

He holds a gold vajra hooked knife with a blade of meteoric iron.

This is primordial wakefulness that spontaneously severs

All thoughts of selfishness, fear, and arrogance.

Thus in his raised left hand, he offers a skull cup

Filled with the pure golden essence of life,

Which is completely free from all the hallucinatory deceptions of life and death.

Radiant and powerful, he is entirely unassuming.

Encountering him, one is comforted

And feels that one is possibly a warrior.

3

The Rigden Mahipala is the life force of all the Rigdens.

In his unchanging inner form, he is deep red like a dawn sun.

He is youthful and at ease and his kindly gaze lights the world.

His smile transforms space itself.

Because rigpa and space are inseparable,

He wears a crown surmounted by a blue diamond.

Because rigpa and action are simultaneous,

This gold crown is adorned with sapphires and emeralds.

Because the boundless space of unceasing great compassion

Is the spontaneous complete fulfillment of all action,

His top-knot is adorned with a blazing emerald.

Thus limitless pure realms spontaneously appear.

So streamers, white on the outside and blue on the inside,

Billow from the sides of his crown.

He wears earrings, necklaces, arm bands, bracelets and anklets.

He is adorned with all the gold and jewels of the world.

Because he enters into every action,

He wears a flowing green shawl of peacock feathers.

A pulsing aureole of soft and red light surrounds his head.

As love and rigpa inseparable pervade every realm.

In his right hand at the level of his heart,

He holds a golden vase surmounted by the three jewels blazing,

The living gift of unconditional fearlessness.

In his right hand, he holds the stem of a pink lotus

On which rests the gold disc of the Great Eastern Sun,

The gift of unceasing inspiration.

He wears orange silk pants embroidered with flowers

And a blue silk skirt embroidered with clouds

He sits on a moon disc that rests on the golden anthers

Of a pink lotus, vast as the heart of compassion,

Blooming spontaneously on the boundless surface of the cosmic mirror itself.

His consort, seated on his right, white as purity itself,

Offers a golden bowl of jewels and every form of richness.

Together they sit amid a whirling blue rainbow

That fills all of existence from the depth of hell to the summit of heaven.

He is uncontrived wakefulness and compassion beyond duality.

He is the heart and realm of every being.

Thus he binds the vast range of pure Buddha fields

To the profundity of the Rigden Kings.

*

THE BRILLIANT SUCCESSION OF THE LORDS OF KALAPA

II.4.24

RIGDEN SRIPALA

1

Now, the seventeenth Rigden of Shambhala, Sripala,

The Glorious Protector, Annihilator of Hosts of Demons,

Appears in the Crystal Pavilion of the Kalapa Court.

He is the emanation of the Lord of Dralas.

2

In a windy, rock-strewn, narrow valley, high in the mountains,

The Rigden Sripala sits on the gold eight lion throne of Shambhala.

He is youthful and his face is very pale and silvery.

His eyes are jet black and his gaze is tender yet ruthless,

As he looks across the plains filled with golden wheat,

Out past the gleaming roofs of Kalapa to the dark horizon beyond.

His slender body is delicate, yet his posture is that of a great warrior.

His black hair is swept back.

He wears the gold crown of a dharma king,

Surmounted by a black diamond emitting rays of black light.

He wears a dark blue silk robe embroidered in silver with thrashing dragons.

His inner robe is the color of steel.

His silk sash is crimson.

He wears a pure white scarf of heavy satin.

He wears the gold necklace and earrings of an earth protector.

Because the blinding radiance of complete wakefulness

Cannot be caught in the half-lights of momentary advantage,

With his right hand on his knee, he shows the gold vajra sword

With its glowing blade of molten meteoric iron.

This is the weapon that destroys aggression.

Because nothing can penetrate, sway or seduce

The complete brilliance of limitless compassion,

In his left hand, he holds the three-pointed khatvanga

Adorned with three severed heads in three states of decay,

Which are the three times themselves.

Encountering him is like being cut through

By a razor knife.

It is done before one can cry out or run.

3

The Rigden Sripala is the self-existing protection of all the Rigdens.

In his unchanging inner form he is blue-black like fathomless space.

His three eyes stare out with objectless fury,

And the razor fangs in his huge gaping mouth

Gnash against his golden lower lip.

Because his all-consuming compassion is not limited by space,

His blazing red hair swirls like the world-ending holocaust.

211

It is bound into a top-knot and held in place by three dried skulls,

Which is the complete exhaustion of time.

Because dharmata has been completely exhausted,

He wears no crown.

He is the source of dharmas,

And so wears a pure white outer robe lined in red and a crimson inner robe.

He is the alaya and abode of the bijas,

And so is adorned with writhing serpents at his waist and neck.

He is the limitless ayatanas,

And wears sparkling gold necklaces and earrings.

Just the sight of him cuts ignorance, passion and aggression to the root;

So in his raised right hand, he brandishes a trident of meteoric iron.

Its handle is carved from a dragon's tooth

And is adorned with a tiger's tail, a lion's mane and a garuda feather,

Because this is the realization of the four dignities, spontaneous and complete.

Because he offers all that is life itself,

In his left hand at the level of his heart, he holds a kapala

Vast as space and boiling with the living essence of the dharmadhatu.

Because complete offering automatically subdues the myriad powers of madness and self-absorption,

In the same hand, he holds a diamond noose that chokes the neck of a naked demon.

There is no power in the world of knowledge which can resist him,

So with his right foot, huge as the earth and sky,

He presses down on the head and hands of a worldly prince.

His throne, with its gilded ebony and cinnabar back,

Bright as the last sunset and the first dawn,

Rests in a great cart drawn by seven elephants:

Two white, two blue, and three black,

Whose power is like untamed mind.

Flying through space on four eight-spoked sapphire wheels.

Its sparks are the stars.

His consort, standing on his left, is dark green like a jungle night.

She wears a crown of five dried skulls, and her three eyes are rapturous.

She wears a freshly flayed human skin around her neck,

And stamps her feet with a thundering sound that breaks the sky.

Her hands move with ceaseless delicacy

In the movements of inviting and dispelling.

His burning radiance cannot be limited, seen, or comprehended.

Thus he binds the dwelling place of all the Buddhas of the three times

To the brilliance of the Rigden Kings.

*

THE BRILLIANT SUCCESSION OF THE LORDS OF KALAPA

II.4.25

RIGDEN HARI

1

Now, the eighteenth Rigden of Shambhala, Hari,

The Holy One, The Remover Who Subdues the Elephant With His Vajra,

Enters the Crystal Pavilion of the Kalapa Court.

He is the emanation of Vajrapani.

2

Beside a cold deep stream on a dry rolling plain,

The Rigden Hari sits on the gold eight-lion throne of Shambhala.

He is youthful and his face is bright gold, smooth and plump.

His eyes are lavender and his gaze is penetrating and all-embracing

His expression is both severe and humorous.

His body is heavy and yet he is very graceful and precise.

His black hair is oiled and perfumed.

He wears the gold crown of a dharma king

In whose summit is set a sapphire whose blue light is like the sky.

He wears a deep orange silk robe embroidered with gold tigers consuming their prey.

His inner robe is black watered silk.

His satin sash is the color of turquoise.

He wears the gold necklace and earrings of an earth protector.

Because neither deception nor self deception can penetrate

The diamond-like expanse of primordially pure mind,

In his right hand, at the level of his heart,

He holds a gold five-pointed vajra.

With his left hand, he rings a golden bell

Whose sound cuts through all the murky shifts of selfishness

And fills the whole of space with light.

Encountering him, one is known inescapably,

And instantly knows oneself.

3

The Rigden Hari is the self-existing light of all the Rigdens.

In his unchanging inner form, he is the color of molten gold.

He is eternally youthful and at ease.

His gaze is discerning and benevolent.

Because empty awareness is always manifest in the world of form,

He wears a gold stupa in his top-knot.

Because the mind of nowness is naked and immediate,

He is not adorned with any crown.

Because non-thought is slain in the natural state,

He wears the skin of an azure antelope around his neck.

Because actions rising in nowness are an infinite treasury,

He wears a necklace, bracelets and anklets

Of gold, emerald and sapphire beads.

Because he brings thoughts and actions to correct completion,

He wears a dark green emerald shawl which moves like the wind itself.

He holds in his right hand the stem of the ever opening blue lotus of rigpa

On which stands the silver staff of command.

Thus justice cuts through all forms of deceit

With the radiance of spontaneous awareness.

In his left hand, he holds the stem of the ever opening pink lotus of limitless compassion,

On which stands a vase filled with amrita

Which intoxicates the madness of selfish craving.

His two hands are joined together in the mudra of endless guidance.

He wears red silk pants embroidered with every kind of bird and animal,

And because his being rises from the spontaneous radiance of compassion itself,

He sits on a moon disc that rests on the green anthers of a vast pink lotus.

There he resides in a six-sided pavilion made of gold, coral and ebony.

Its roof is gold and surmounted by the blazing three jewels.

Amongst the many treasures in his pavilion

Is a golden dharmachakra which emits rays of rainbow wisdom light as it rotates

And a conch whose turning binds the world of the senses and the
elements.

On his right, his consort is white and luminous

As the full moon reflected on a black lake.

She wears the crown of complete enjoyment made from pink
lotuses

And holds the ensign of Shambhala victory

Made from peacock feathers in the shape of a bodhi leaf.

It bears a picture of a Rigden spreading jewels

As he rides across the earth on his horse of miracles.

The pavilion and its occupants are supported by eight dakinis,

Dancing playfully in the clouds.

He is the spontaneous union of thought and non-thought;

Thus he binds the pure radiant light of all the Buddhas

As the justice of the Rigden Kings.

*

II.4.26

RIGDEN VIKRAMA

1

Now, the nineteenth Rigden of Shambhala, Vikrama,

The Complete Conqueror, He Who Subdues Of All Outer and Inner Demons,

Takes his seat in the Crystal Pavilion of the Kalapa Court.

He is the emanation of Yamantaka.

2

In the cinnabar throne room of Shambhala

As the gilt-work glows softly in the lengthening shadows of autumn,

The Rigden Vikrama sits on the gold eight-lion throne of Shambhala.

Though he is in middle age, his face is smooth and clean-shaven.

His skin is the color of bronze, and his eyes are pale blue.

His expression is sad but fearless, and his gaze fills the air

With an atmosphere of complete steadfastness.

His body is powerful and all his movements are deliberate.

His black hair is combed back.

He wears the gold brocade turban and gold crown of a dharma king

219

In whose apex is set an emerald

Which glows as if alive.

His outer robe is white silk brocade adorned with golden lions leaping to attack.

His inner robe is made of spun gold.

His silk sash is pale saffron.

He wears the gold necklace and earrings of an earth protector.

Because the absolute and relative truth can not be separated,

He wields the power of time and cannot be opposed;

So in his right hand, he holds up a mace of meteoric iron.

Because on the vast mirror of the unborn,

All beings journey between life and death.

None can escape the cycles of the seasons, nor of cause and effect.

Therefore, in his left hand, he holds a noose made of diamond chain.

Encountering him,

One feels the beauty and the oppression of being alive.

The Rigden Vikrama is the unsought power of all the Rigdens.

In his unchanging inner form,

He is the glowing orange of a blacksmith's fire.

His body is powerful and taut like a bow.

His three eyes are awareness itself,

And his gaze passes through the shadows of life and death.

His red lips are closed in a throb of passion.

He is what continues, and so his hair, red and flickering

Like the warmth of love, the heat of sustenance,

And the flames of the cremation pyre,

Is bound into a top-knot unadorned.

Because this is the knowledge of eternity,

The spontaneous union of wisdom and compassion,

He wears a gold crown adorned with sapphires and rubies.

Because even the wild yearning for living cannot overcome him,

He wears the skin of a pregnant tigress around his waist.

Because he is alive in every moment of birth, life and death,

He wears a gray serpent round his neck

Whose head and tail embrace at the level of his secret center.

Serpents and gold chains adorn his wrists, arms, ankles.

He wears a necklace of gold and every kind of gem,

And a green silk scarf swirls everywhere from around his neck.

Because the power of reality

Stabs through the heart and breaks the back

Of all the delusory creations of passion, aggression and ignorance,

In his right hand he holds a razor-sharp blue vajra trident.

Because this is the weapon of innate purity,

It is adorned by a white scarf of pure white silk.

A river of rainbow light emanates from the tips of his trident

And forms a vast turning gold dharma chakra,

As the power of truth becomes law and deliverance.

In his left hand, he holds a gold vajra Khatvanga

Below which hang three skulls in three states of decay.

This is the transformation of all thought

Into the three Kayas, the fulfillment in bliss of the path of Buddhadharma.

The staff which supports the trident on the right

And that which supports the khatvanga on the left

Are red and white because these powers are the constituent of the human body.

Because his movement is the energy of reality itself,

His throne has a gilded red and blue cloud back

Held in the mouth of the Lord of Death.

His throne is a cinnabar and gold chariot

With four all-accomplishing emerald eight-spoked wheels.

It is drawn through the misty clouds of infinite space by seven great garudas

Whose bodies are red and whose faces and wings are green and blue.

His consort, standing on his left, is blue like pure night sky.

She holds the gold vajra of indestructible wisdom in her right hand

And in her left, the silver bell which is compassion, spontaneously complete.

She wears a shawl, white on the inside red on the outside

Because she is the origin, development and end of all.

He is the utter inseparability of absolute and relative truth,

Of rigpa and its innate radiance, great compassion,

Thus he binds the seat of all the Buddhas

To the power of all the Rigden Kings.

RIGDEN MAHABALA

1

Now, the twentieth Rigden of Shambhala, Mahabala,

Great Strength, He Who Tames False Leaders With Mantra,

Enters the Crystal Pavilion of the Kalapa Court.

He is the emanation of Kshitigharba.

2

Beside a cold black mountain lake, in a valley filled with juniper,

The Rigden Mahabala sits on the gold eight-lion throne of Shambhala.

He is youthful and his smooth face is pale gold.

His features are delicate, almost feminine and his eyes are obsidian black.

His gaze is sharp and clever, but his expression is unreadable.

His body is wiry, and he sits unmoving in the posture of a great warrior.

His shiny black hair is combed back.

He wears the gold brocade turban and gold crown of a dharma king

Surmounted by a radiant clear diamond which illuminates the whole room.

His outer robe is red silk embroidered with golden garudas wheeling through clouds.

He wears a cape of black sable fur.

His sash is white satin.

He wears earrings and a necklace adorned with a gold and iron wheel of an earth protector.

In his right hand on his knee, he plays an ivory damaru,

Alternating soft subtle rhythms with sudden sharp attacks,

As his wishes, inseparable from the movements of the sun itself,

Move in the air like breezes, gusts, shouts, eddies, whispers, drafts.

In his left hand at his hip, he holds a mass of blazing jewels,

Radiant with the light of true command.

Encountering him, one has many doubts,

But everything that one should do seems very clear.

3

The Rigden Mahabala is the irresistible strength of all the Rigdens.

In his unchanging inner form, he is blue as a sapphire, radiant and transparent.

His body is eternally youthful and rests at ease.

His gaze is steady but touches everything that moves

His coral lips are curved in a subtle smile.

Because he is the lord whose intentions are carried out in every passion,

He wears the gold and jeweled crown of the five families.

Because everything that passes in his mind is spontaneously fulfilled,

His crown is surmounted by a blazing great blue diamond and flanked by two blazing emeralds

He wears a garland of red and white lotuses reaching to his secret center.

Because the vastness of purity and the vastness of compassion

Are inseparable and are bliss itself.

He wears gold earrings, necklaces, armbands, bracelets and anklets,

Because bliss is permanent and all-pervasive.

He wears a billowing silk shawl, green on the outside, red on the inside

As his being pervades all the movements of the earth, of thought, and beyond thought.

In his right hand, he holds the green stem of a white lotus in full bloom

On which stands gold five-pointed vajra,

The free and indestructible essence which, without moving,

Destroys all that is not genuine from within.

In his left hand, he holds the green stem of a white lotus in full bloom

On which stands a gold and silver bell,

The radiant and infinite expanse of bliss in which all delusions inescapably dissolve.

He holds his two hands together at the level of his heart in the gesture of turning the wheel,

As vajra and bell twine in the ever unfolding dance of mudra and mantra.

He wears orange silk pants adorned with gold mountains and gold lakes.

He wears a red silk skirt embroidered in gold and silver clouds, moons, stars and suns.

He sits on a pure moon disc which rests on the saffron anthers of an immense lotus

Whose petals are white and fleshy and whose tips are pink.

This rests in turn on a circular throne of gold, cinnabar and lapis

Which is held aloft by eight worldly deities.

His consort, blue as the sky before dawn, sits at his right,

And plays the vina, flooding the world with the endless play of sound.

Together, they sit amid a great mass of rainbow light

Which fills the three worlds and bathes the five-tiered Palace of Kalapa behind them.

From a gold stupa behind the palace, the great mandala of Kalachakra

Spontaneously emanates on a swirl of gold and ruby light.

It hovers in the air visible to all.

He is innate, unceasing, vibrant, all-pervasive and all accomplishing.

Thus he binds the bliss of acting as desired enjoyed by all the Buddhas of the three times,

To the All Victoriousness of all the Rigden Kings.

*

THE BRILLIANT SUCCESSION OF THE LORDS OF KALAPA

II.4.28

RIGDEN ANIRUDDHA

1

Now, the twenty-first Rigden of Shambhala, Aniruddha,

The Unobstructed, He Who Drives and Binds the Three Worlds,

Emerges in the Crystal Hall of the Kalapa Court.

He is the emanation of Vajrakilaya.

2

In the cool throne room of Kalapa, glowing in the afternoon light,

The Rigden Aniruddha sits on the gold eight-lion throne of Shambhala.

He is youthful in the taut eagerness of early adolescence.

His face is smooth and the color of white jade.

His features are strong and his eyes are bright blue.

His gaze is direct and watchful and his expression restrained and sincere.

His body is stocky and he sits erect.

His discipline and simplicity are impressive.

His hair is black, very fine, and combed back beneath his crown.

He wears the gold crown of a dharma king

Which is surmounted by a fathomless sapphire.

His outer robe is saffron-colored, embroidered in gold with dancing tigers.

His inner robe is heavy dark blue silk.

His sash is the color of turquoise.

He wears the gold earrings and necklace of an earth protector.

In his right hand, he holds a gilded vajra goad aloft

Driving all who linger in laziness, doubt and hesitation

Into the unsparing light of the Great Eastern Sun.

In his left hand at his waist, he holds an iron chain with hook and noose.

Thus he binds all secret fears and covert arrogance

To the path of limitless confidence.

Encountering him, one feels challenged

To greater exertion and greater openness.

3

The Rigden Aniruddha is the unobstructed action of all the Rigdens.

In his unchanging inner form, he is white as a peaceful new moon.

His body is youthful and very still.

His gaze is unswerving and completely penetrating.

The smile on his lips is loving and unbiased.

In the limitless vastness of his mind,

All movement is primordial wisdom light;

Thus he wears the gold crown of the five families.

And because his unceasing love fulfills all the cycles of time,

His Crown is surmounted by a ruby which blazes a halo of intense red light.

His crown is adorned with silk streamers, green on the outside, red on the inside

Because love and complete accomplishment are inseparable.

Because all that arises from the red and white elements and their joining is completely pure,

A garland of red and white lotuses in full bloom encircles his entire body.

He wears a gold and jeweled necklaces, armbands and earrings

Since the poverty of ego-fixation is completely dispelled.

He wears a billowing shawl, green on the outside and blue on the inside

Since in his all-pervasive vastness, every dharma is completely accomplished.

In his right hand, he holds aloft a golden vajra goad

With a blade of meteoric iron.

Thus when the inherent aggression

Of all thoughts and subconscious gossip are subdued,

The vastness of the ayatanas unfolds as an immeasurable still
lake.

His vajra goad is adorned with a silk streamer, red on the outside
and blue on the inside

Because mirror-like awareness and compassion are inseparable.

In his left hand, he holds, at the level of his heart,

A long diamond chain ending in an iron hook and noose.

So he binds all seeming obstacles to the path.

Thus all is united in the golden ocean of the Rigdens' mind.

Because he moves spontaneously through the entire sky of mind,

He wears rainbow silk pants.

He sits on a jade disc in the center of a gold and cinnabar
circular throne.

His consort kneeling on his right is white as a conch

And holds her hands in the angeli of reverence and peace.

Together they sit amid a rainbow of gold light

Pervading the whole of time.

He is the life-force of primordial peace

And unites the vajra karma

To the dignity of meek of all the Rigden Kings.

*

THE BRILLIANT SUCCESSION OF THE LORDS OF KALAPA

II.4.29

RIGDEN NARISIMSHA

1

Now, the twenty-second Rigden of Shambhala, Narisimha,

Man-Lion, Destroyer of Demons, Having the Power of Vishnu,

Not Subject to the Limits of Human or Animal Realms,

Ruling by the Wheel and Holder of the Conch,

Appears in the Crystal Pavilion of the Kalapa Court.

He is the emanation of Sarvanivaranaviskrambin.

2

High among the frozen peaks surrounding Kalapa, beside a
frozen lake,

The Rigden Narisimha sits on the gold eight-lion throne of
Shambhala.

233

He is in the full strength of early middle age, and his face is very dark.

His features are heavy, and his eyes are yellow.

His expression is fierce and exultant,

And beneath his thick curved eyebrows, his gaze is restless and sharp.

His body is heavy and powerful like a resting lion

Enjoying the mere presence of his innate power,

And knowing that his immense strength can focus in a flash.

His thick black mustache, beard and hair are oiled and smooth.

He wears the gold brocade turban and gold crown of a dharma king

On whose peak a yellow and black gzhi seems to pulse and writhe.

His outer robe is pearl white embroidered with gold lions devouring prey.

His silk sash is deep orange like an autumn sun.

His black boots are polished antelope skin.

He wears the heavy gold earrings of an earth protector.

In his right hand at the level of his secret center,

He holds a gold eight-spoked wheel,

And as he turns it in his hand, the vowels and consonants

Pierce the cocoon of self-absorption and fill the whole of space

234

With the ceaseless melody of true law.

In his left hand, he holds a great white conch shell aloft

Whose trumpet sounds completely intoxicate all false views

And paralyze all conflicting emotions.

Encountering him, one knows that one can be destroyed on the spot.

3

The Rigden Narisimha is the fearless warrior joy of all the Rigdens.

In his unchanging inner form, he is translucent white and filled with light

Like a cold mist in sunlight.

His body is very youthful and completely at ease.

His dark eyes penetrate all phenomena,

And his gaze rests in fathomless space.

His effortless smile is that of one who is completely victorious.

Because all wisdom is complete in action,

He wears the gold and five-jewel crown of the Tathagathas.

Because his ceaseless activity is complete non-dual compassion,

His black hair is bound into a top-knot with a red silk cord and surmounted by a blazing emerald.

His head is surrounded by a halo the deep red color of a dawning sun.

Because his love is all consuming,

He wears a red mantle and red silk pants adorned with gold swirling galaxies.

As he spontaneously resolves all thoughts to non-thought bliss,

The skin of a lapis-colored antelope, freshly killed,

Is draped over his left shoulder.

He wears necklaces, bracelets and earrings of gold and jewels

Because all the gates to the lower realms are completely transformed.

A long scarf, green on the outside, red on the inside, billows around him,

As his love sweeps through the three times.

In his right hand, open in the gesture of offering,

He holds the green stem of a red lotus in full bloom

On which stands the golden eight-spoked dharmachakra

Whose all-pervasive light burns the castles of the maras and destroys all doubts.

In his left hand he holds the green stem of a pink lotus

On which stands a conch the color of moonlight.

The great winds of life, swirling through this shell

Reduce all solid-seeming forms to the radiance of pure perception.

He also holds a diamond chain with hook and noose of meteoric iron

Which captures, subdues and binds all the calculations of demons and heretics

Into the unfabricated freedom of dharmadhatu wisdom.

His square throne, sitting on the earth element itself,

Is gold, ebony and cinnabar,

And is supported by the worldly deities of wisdom and wealth.

His consort sitting on his right is the red and golden color of a forest fire.

She offers a wish-fulfilling jewel the color of sapphire.

Together they sit in a whirling mass of blue rainbow light,

Pervading the sky, the seas, the earth as utter fearlessness.

He is the spontaneous reality of complete enlightenment

And unites the all accomplishing karma

To the dignity of perky of all the Rigden Kings.

*

THE BRILLIANT SUCCESSION OF THE LORDS OF KALAPA

II.4.30

RIGDEN MAHESVARA

1

Emerging from the Kalapa Court of the Kalapa Court

Comes the twenty-third Rigden of Shambhala, Mahesvara,

Lord of the World, possessor of Siva's powers,

Victorious Over Armies of Demons.

He is the emanation of Akashagharba.

2

In the warm gilded cinnabar throne room of Kalapa,

Whose windows look out on thin clouds drifting in the cold empty air,

The Rigden Mahesvara sits on the gold eight-lion throne of Shambhala.

He is in the full strength of early manhood, and his pale face is flushed.

His features are sharp and refined,

And the pupils of his eyes glow like rubies.

His gaze embraces all the world and beyond the world.

His expression is blissful.

His body is slender, and as he sits, he is vibrant but at ease.

His thin mustache and light beard are black and his hair is
combed back.

He wears the gold crown of a dharma king

At whose peak a ruby glows like a distant fire.

His outer robe is red embroidered in gold with flying garudas.

His inner robe is made from spun pale gold.

His silk sash is the color of a mountain glacier.

He wears the gold necklace and earrings of an earth protector.

In his right hand resting on his knee,

He holds the stem of a red lotus in full bloom

On which stands the flaming vajra sword,

The wisdom which rises spontaneously in the vastness
motiveless compassion

And instantly discriminates the path of basic goodness.

In his left hand on his knee,

He holds the eight-metal shield with eight ribs adorned with a
lion's mane,

The self-existing protection of the eight-fold path.

Encountering him, one feels inflamed

By the boundlessness of passion.

The Rigden Mahesvara is the fearless vast commitment of all the Rigdens.

In his unchanging inner form, he is deep blue like a winter night.

He is very youthful and his body is at ease.

His gaze is boundless and impartial like the sky itself.

His moist red lips do not smile but are completely welcoming.

Because he is all-pervasive in light or dark, sleep, dream or waking life,

His crown is woven from the fragrant blue utpala flower.

Because he is all-pervasive in action and thought,

A blazing sapphire and two blazing emeralds are woven in this crown.

Because all that can be realized has been realized completely,

His hair is in the shape of an usnisha.

Because in the world, he is experienced as unbounded passion,

Red silk ribbons flutter from his crown,

And because he is boundless life,

A gold-red halo radiates from around his head.

As the originator of the vowels and consonants,

He wears a garland of red and white lotuses in full bloom.

As the radiance and pulse of all phenomena,

He wears gold necklaces, anklets, bracelets and earrings.

Because he is the essence of life and death,

He wears a vast shawl, black on the outside, red on the inside.

Because he moves in the whole domain of space,

He wears silk rainbow-colored pants.

In his right hand, he holds aloft the full moon of compassion,

Ever clear and bright, reflecting everywhere

And lighting a path in darkness

Even as it sails across the earth on clouds.

In his left hand, he holds the stem of the pink lotus

Of inseparable purity and compassion

On which stands the blazing three jewels,

The innate refuge of rigpa, luminosity and compassion.

He sits in the light of all, on a moon and sun disc

Which rests on a blue and green lotus vast as reality.

Seated on his left, his consort, gold as the life-giving sun,

Offers a conch filled with the water of deathless commitment.

They are surrounded by an immense vibrant rainbow of light,

The light of form and formless bliss in the three times and the three worlds.

They are drawn on their lotus throne on great white clouds

Through all the reach and range of space by seven great steeds,

One the color of lapis, one that is copper-colored, one the color of turquoise,

Two the color of pearl, and two the color of bronze.

They trample over the demons of hope and fear,

And open the measureless empty radiant space of selfless love.

He is the unmoving all-pervading union of bliss and space,

And unites the karma of spontaneous discrimination

To the dignity of outrageousness of all the Rigden Kings.

*

THE BRILLIANT SUCCESSION OF THE LORDS OF KALAPA

II.4.31

RIGDEN ANANTAVIJAYA

1

Now, the twenty-fourth Rigden of Shambhala, Anantavijaya,

Limitless Victory, The Holder of Vajra and Ghanta

Takes his seat in the Crystal Pavilion of the Kalapa Court.

He is the emanation of Vajrapani.

2

In the cold vermilion shrine room of the Kalapa Court,

Wreathed in coils of juniper smoke and the steam of his own breath,

The Rigden Anantavijaya sits on the gold eight-lion throne of Shambhala.

He is in late middle age and his face is the color of polished bronze.

His features are strong and elegant, and his large eyes are gold.

His gaze is precise and settled, without avidity or gap in his attention.

His expression is non-committal yet gently humorous.

His body is powerful and unwavering, like a great oak tree.

His mustache is trim and his dark hair is combed back.

He wears the gold brocade turban and crown of a dharma king

Surmounted by a green pulsing wish-fulfilling gem.

His outer robe is blue silk embroidered in gold with sinuous dragons.

His inner robe is emerald-colored.

His silk sash is crimson, the color of heart's blood.

He wears the lavish golden earrings of an earth protector.

His boots are made from the iridescent skin of a serpent and shod in gold.

He sits with his left leg slightly extended.

Because his heart is inseparable from the light of changeless space,

In his right hand at the level of his heart, he extends a golden five-pointed vajra.

Because his heart is inseparable from the infinite dance of time,

In his left hand, he holds a ghanta with a golden vajra stem and a silver bell upturned.

Encountering him, one feels awed by unconditional freedom,

And cannot tell whether it is his or one's own.

3

The Rigden Anantavijaya is the complete freedom of all the Rigdens.

In his unchanging inner form, he is primordially youthful.

He is stainless white like the essence of space.

His gaze is gentle and unwavering,

And his lips curve slightly in a humorous smile.

Because he resolves all forms of aggression in the three times,

His hair, the color of a vast peaceful sea, is bound in an ushisha.

Because boundless love rises and is fulfilled in complete peace,

His usnisha is adorned with a golden Buddha

Emanating red light from his body and blue light from his head.

Because, devoid of struggle or calculation,

His mind is complete, passionless non-thought,

He wears no crown, but the red light of unconditional love

Emanates from around his head filling the form and formless
worlds.

All the realms of poverty and hunger are spontaneously
overcome,

And so he wears a short cloak of pure gold, luminous as a golden
sea.

The cloak is lined with the pink of unswerving gentleness.

He wears sapphires and emeralds around his neck on a red silk
cord.

And because his gifts pervade the solid world,

He wears earrings, bracelets and anklets of heavy solid gold.

Unobstructed by empty space or illusory phenomena,

He wears a billowing shawl, black on the outside, azure on the
inside.

Because he incites all the movements of the elements,

And restores in time all phenomena to their innate purity,

In his right hand he holds aloft a vajra goad,

Gold with a blade of meteoric iron

And adorned with a blue and white scarf.

Because with the chain of the vowels and consonants,

He spontaneously binds all the raging torments of false conception

To the wisdom of their radiant display,

In his left hand he holds a diamond chain with golden hook and noose.

He wears red silk pants adorned with galaxies of golden stars,

A blue skirt adorned with silver clouds and a green and black sash.

He sits on the glowing moon disk of limitless compassion

Which rests on the green field of winds

In the center of the vast pink lotus of all phenomena

Alive, pulsing in full bloom.

His consort seated on his right is the color of a yellow pearl,

And she extends the crystal bowl of limitless offering.

They sit amid a vibrant golden rainbow, vast as the ayatanas themselves,

Pervading all worlds, realms and times with the richness of
innate freedom.

He is ultimate warriorship, the fearlessness of the mind lineage

Shining in the limitlessness of the ayatanas.

Thus he unites the karma of destroying

To the dignity of inscrutable of all the Rigden Kings.

*

THE BRILLIANT SUCCESSION OF THE LORDS OF KALAPA

RIGDEN RAUDRACAKRIN

1

Now, the twenty-fifth Rigden of Shambhala, Raudracakrin,

The Wrathful One Who Turns The Wheel,

He Who Ends the Current Time of Strife and Establishes a
Golden Age,

Takes command of the Crystal Pavilion of the Kalapa Court.

He is the emanation of Vajrakilaya.

In the middle of his army, as in a tumult of gold and turquoise clouds,

Seated on his great blue charger with blue-black mane and tail,

Whose gold ornaments glitter, filling the sky with lightning bolts

And whose stamping hooves shake the earth with thunder,

The Rigden Raudracakrin emerges from the fastness of Kalapa

And bursts into the world of time,

Cutting to the heart of cowardice.

He is in the prime of manhood, and his face is and body are dark red.

His obsidian eyes glare with imperious fury and he snarls with rage.

He wears the dazzling gold crown of a dharma king

Adorned with glowing emeralds and sapphires.

His golden armor is blinding like the direct sight of the sun.

Around his neck, on a white silk scarf, he wears a crystal mirror

In which all the phenomena of time and space arise and dissolve.

Beneath his armor, he wears a robe of green brocade with red sleeves lined in pale coral satin.

His pants are made of red brocade adorned with golden dragons.

His gold-shod boots are made of red and white brocade.

A great lapis-colored serpent twines round his neck falling to the level of his secret center.

Green serpents trailing dark clouds encircle his wrists.

In his right hand raised aloft, he brandishes the flaming spear

Which destroys the universe with kalpa-ending fire.

The shaft of his spear is adorned with garudas' feathers

And a swirling green and coral scarf.

In his left hand, he spins the eight-pointed wheel of meteoric iron

Marked with eight great syllables, whose sound, as the wheel turns,

Destroys all false beliefs about reality and deafens all the emotions of grasping and fixation.

At the sight of him, worlds perish and are reborn.

3

The Rigden Raudracakrin is the complete manifestation of all the Rigdens.

In his unchanging secret form, he is the great protector, Manjusri.

Youthful and at ease, his red body is the color of an all-consuming sandal-wood fire.

Nothing in the form and formless worlds, in mind and beyond mind

Is separate from the light of his unwavering empty gaze.

All distortions, upheavals, displays, realizations and search for freedom

Resolve within his sovereign equipoise.

All the winds of sky and earth are his soft voice,

The secret speech of Samantabhadra.

Because he is the complete lord of all wisdom,

He wears the gold and jeweled crown of the five Tathagathas

Because wisdom presence is inseparable from limitless compassion,

His crown is surmounted by a ruby the size of Mount Meru.

Because his light shines out in all phenomena,

He wears necklaces, arm bands, bracelets and anklets

Of shining gold and glittering jewels.

Because he enters into all the world's activities,

He wears a billowing shawl of shimmering emerald green.

His skirt is coral and adorned with golden butterflies.

His red silk pants are adorned with galaxies of suns and moons,

And their blue lining is embroidered with all the swirling clouds in space.

In his right hand, held at his heart in the mudra of teaching,

He holds the green stem of a fragrant pink lotus in full bloom

On which stand the gold eight-spoked wheel of the law turning in a mass of flame.

By the turning of the wheel, the claustrophobia of illusory reality

Is shown to be inseparable from all-pervasive, free, luminous bliss.

In his left hand, held at his heart in the mudra of ceaseless offering,

He holds the green stem of a vast pink lotus in full bloom

On which stands the blazing sword of primordial awareness

Which spontaneously cuts through the pained half-light of conceptualization

And reveals on the spot the infinite radiant empty space of liberation.

He is seated on a hexagonal, cloud-backed throne of gold and cinnabar

Supported by eight snow-lions.

Above him a gold and vermilion parasol sways,

Adorned with garlands of gold beads, jewels, silver bells and silk banners.

To his right, his consort, green Sarasvati, plays the Vina

Flooding all of space with melodious sound.

To his left, his consort white as the full moon of compassion,

In her hands in angeli at her heart holds the stem of a white lotus in full bloom

On which stands the sharp sword of omniscience.

They traverse the sky amid sky palaces and offering devis,

And are surrounded by rainbows of light which are every kind of knowing.

He is the complete spontaneous and ever-present power of wisdom,

The deathless Ashe, the inseparability of space and awareness,

The resolution of time and space,

The life force essence of all the Rigden Kings.

4

When time in this realm began,

The world was filled with jewel seas

Surrounding the four great and eight lesser continents

Ranged around Mount Meru.

All the consciousness of beings dwelt in bodies of pure light.

But fascinated by compounded phenomena,

And grasping at continuity,

Beings encased themselves in solidity.

Confidence in the power of egoless action waned.

The three lords of materialism grew in strength

And came to appear to humans as transcendental gods.

Only deities who promised man's dominion were supplicated.

Only philosophies seeking exclusive human happiness were pursued.

Beginning then in the time of Rigden Samudravijaya

These philosophies and faiths assumed a single face

In the doctrines of the La-los. Madhumati became supreme.

In the following 1700 years, Central Asia, India, China, the Middle East

And more than half the entire world fell beneath its sway.

The earth was then robbed as an unattended treasure house.

The seas became mere fisheries and middens.

Rivers were dammed and lakes used as farms.

Fire became merely a source of household comfort and mechanical power.

The air was fouled.

Forests and plains were destroyed or cultivated according to human need.

Birds, fish, and animals were hunted, captured, butchered and skinned.

The geography of the earth itself assumed hallucinatory shapes.

This is the time of disputes and poisons.

In the headlong race for material gain,

Civilizations and cultures collapse from within and without.

Nations, villages and families split.

Parent and child, brother and sister, life-long friends

Become murderous enemies.

Parents prostitute their children.

Plagues corrupt love and poison water and air.

Insane murderous tyrants, surrounded by cruel lustful
sycophants,

Shall rule the earth by the power of terror alone.

Power, violence, scheming and raw possession shall be the only
good.

Famine, disease and warfare shall be the only truth.

Nobility, compassion, decency, gentleness, courage

Shall be only words in books.

The world shall be a burning prison house without solace or
liberation.

Drugged hallucinations shall be the only refuge.

Drang Tzi Lodro, the La-lo King, will unify his forces and tribes
at Tri-Li in Central India.

Then incited by the words of his queen, he will, like a maddened
elephant,

Press to conquer all the worlds beyond his own.

Hearing of Shambhala, and seeing it in the smoke of incense
offered to his god,

He will mass his armies.

At the same time, like the stench of a rotting corpse,

The vapors from this world

Will begin to poison the air of Shambhala itself.

The dharma will begin to wither and half the abhidharma will disappear.

5

Then, as suddenly as waking up from a murderous nightmare,

As blindingly as seeing the sun appearing in the eye of a black hurricane,

The Rigden Raudracakrin will appear,

Filling the sky with his vast retinue of gods and goddesses,

Generals, ministers, war-carts elephants, cavalry and foot-soldiers.

He will appear in the shining fortress that Mara cannot destroy,

From which the lightning of spontaneous wisdom shatters the black tomb of despair.

Thus ordinary insight will become supreme insight,

Will manifest as the radiant, primordial completion of time. (9)

Though he is the essence of peace,

Though his mind does not move from the peaceful state of dharmata,

And is inseparable from the minds of the three great protectors of all beings,

The Rigden Raudracakrin will appear to those lost in the rats' maze of materialism,

And to their proud, cruel and deceptive leaders

As the wrathful and unbearable gleam of the sun of reality,

Annihilating their path and their very life.   (10)

The dharma lord will then emerge from the city of Kalapa.

In the sky surrounding him will be a great retinue

Of worldly and transcendent gods.

Lion-headed Vishnu, the all-pervading, furious with eyes ablaze,

Will ride out on the back of a fire--red garuda,

Wielding the wheel of time and the sword that severs ignorance.

Brahma, lord of space and time, in his gold and ruby battle cart with pennants fluttering,

Will brandish the bow and golden arrows

That fill the heart with fatal hallucinations of passion and of birth.

Siva, Dark Lord of Rishis, Lord of Night and Dreams,

Will fly on an emerald disc with the sound of thunder rolling across the sky

And wave his trident that penetrates birth, continuing and death.

Kumara Skanda, leader of the army of the gods,

Ever youthful with six faces and six arms,

Will shoot his arrows, hurl his thunderbolts and spears.

As he skims above the earth on the back of a great blue peacock,

Riding in a vermilion and gold chariot

Drawn by blue and white celestial steeds,

He will wield his ax and sword.

The twin Asvin gods, Nasatya and Dasra, lithe, shining and handsome,

Bringers of harvest and health, famine and plague,

Shall destroy the fortunes of the enemy.

Riding within his gold and cinnabar cart floating in the air,

Seated on the great blue mouse which is the enjoyment of all,

Great Ganapati white with six arms and one tusk in his elephant head,

He who Binds the Minute to the Infinite and contains all in his great form,

Shall destroy all false distinctions with his trumpet's scream.

These are the foremost amongst the myriad gods and their retinues

Who will encircle the true dharma and protect it.

Space in all its ten directions will be a protection circle.

At that time, from the unfabricated samadhi which is wind-horse itself,

Joyful, doubtless, genuine and loving,

Spontaneously free from any fixation,

Moving freely in the vast space of the ayatanas,

The Great Dharma Lord, Rigden Raudrachakrin will arise.

He will emanate ninety million stone horses with the power of wind,

Four hundred thousand immense conch-colored elephants, enraged as if drunk,

Five hundred thousand gold chariots and war machines with catapults of fire,

And four vast armies of six million great human warrior lords,

All in splendid golden armor and fully armed.

Among them will ride a host of generals and warriors

Who have the realization of the great lord.

When the great battle begins, the false protectors of the La-los

Dwelling in clouds, mountains and streams will be pierced.

Their powers of illusion will be dispersed like mist.

The Asura Mara Ritha will be pierced through the left side of his head,

By the weapons of the assembled gods.

The Rigden Raudracakrin will pierce the Asura Mara Mati with his spear.

At that very moment, all the holy images and icons of the La-Los

Will shatter into dust.

Rash and arrogant, drunk on their own power of violence,

The La-lo leaders will urge their shaken soldiers on.

The La-lo armies will be torn between hallucinations of defeat

And desperate images of victory until they are in utter disarray and torment.

Rank upon rank, the La-lo troops will be slaughtered,

Crushed under chariot wheels, burned with flames of molten copper,

Pierced with arrows, hacked with swords, and crushed under elephants' feet.

Yet, terrified as they are, they will still be pressed forward

By the men behind who are still more afraid of their own generals.

The carnage will continue unabated for days

Until the Shambhala General Hanumanda slices the throat

Of the La-lo general with his golden sword.

Then all the leaders of darkness shall be one by one struck down.

Finally, the Great Dharma Lord, Rigden Raudrachakrin himself,

Leaning down from the back of his sky blue steed,

Will swing his time-ending spear of meteoric iron in a great arc

And send its razor point down through the skull of the La-lo king.

The spear will penetrate downward through his entire body.

The life thread of the La-lo King and all his followers will be utterly shredded.

They shall be cut down and none will remain.

The La-lo dharma, risen from ignorance and darkness

And causing immeasurable harm and suffering to sentient beings,

Shall be utterly reversed by the power of authentic dharma.

Thus the continuity of non-dharma will be completely cut off.

6

Then, surrounded by his retinue of god and human warriors,

The Dharma Lord Raudracakrin will return to the mountain palace of Kalapa.

He will turn the wheel of dharma throughout the human realm,

And thus complete the time of his reign.

He and all his retinue will then enter the unborn space of the pure realms. (11)

As it has been said:

At that time on the earth, all beings will be one family.

Their minds will be wholesome and all activities fulfilled.

The desire for wealth, sensual enjoyment, dharma and liberation

Shall be completed in their fruition.

Grain will flourish even in deserted places,

The fruit of the trees shall abound.

People will enjoy the fullness of life.

In the eight succeeding generations of Shambhala Rigdens,

The Rigdens will dwell continually in the realms of mahamudra and rigpa.

Their subject will grasp the inner meaning

And dwell with them in the pure expanse of radiant fathomless expanse. (12)

At the conclusion of their reigns,

The dharma shall end in this place.

Until the Buddha of the next eon, Maitreya, shall appear.

Now,

Here,

Unborn space, radiant unconditional awareness, unconditional
compassion

Completely enter the realms of perception, concept, birth and
death,

Encompass infinite colors forms, expressions, sounds.

Now,

Here,

Endless waves of boundless love

Gather, swell, break and dissolve

The night sky was vast and starry. A wisp of juniper smoke scented the air. Gesar felt utterly alone.

THE TIME OF KALAPA

Searching for your heart,

It seems as if

It were a fish deep in a rippling stream,

Even as you see it flash and leap,

You lose sight of it and cannot find its place.

Without even seeming to flex or move,

Even in still water, it is gone.

Staring at an empty pool,

Suddenly smooth and clear, it is right before your eyes

An expanding ripple,

Trembling slowly,

Calling

Moment of space,

Moment of sun and moon and stars,

Moment of sky,

Moment of fire,

Moment of water.

Moment of earth.

Expanding and joining

Each realm as you.

Flickering through the seasons

So rapidly,

So continuously,

So brilliantly,

So fully,

That if you blink,

You may think that this age and world,

Yearning and idea are completely real,

And so may try to live again

Within the dream life of a corpse.

2

In the absolute stillness

At the point of nowness,

Pervasive as light in a mirror

Is this solitary cool remoteness,

Is this delicate joy of intimacy.

While here in this instant,

The unsought powers of the human heart blaze and sparkle

Like the scales of a golden fish

Flashing beneath the surface of a clear black pond.

So the Lords of radiant space

Ride through the skies of time

And open the pathway to the self-arising Shambhala,

The golden heart-realm.

Oh, the subtle winds of space

Oh, the passionate winds of fire

Oh, the clear winds of water

Oh, the enduring winds of earth.

The luminosity of essences,

Great spirits, Great beings

Rise from the edge of time,

Riding winds in a circle of display

We hear:

GARUDA

WHISPERING OF KI

3

S0

Now, the pure heart opens

A circular sea of golden light;

Shows within itself a vast lotus,

A realm, a kingdom

With ranges of misty snow mountains,

Fragrant dark forests, grassy pastures,

Turquoise lakes and glittering streams.

Here at the center, on the highest point,

Vast, brilliant and serene is the Crystal Hall of Kalapa.

From here emerge the Rigdens, one by one,

In armor and brocade with golden crowns.

The face of each is different.

Each displays to you his attributes,

The secret emblem to counter the evils of the age

In which he rules.

The lightning flashes

Reflecting from their helmets, their armor

Their jewels, and their swords,

Are spontaneous songs of now.

They appear one by one,

Each in a blaze of multi-colored light,

Rulers of the past present and future,

Dancing slowly in a circle.

In the immense courtyard of the palace,

Surrounded by crimson colonnades with gilded capitols,

They sway in stately dance.

As their eyes meet yours,

You feel you are drowning in a fathomless lake

Where fear, excitement, hope, self-doubt

Are washed from you,

Even as you drift into a world you have not quite known.

The Queens of the Mother lineage emerge,

With soft smiles and imperial poise,

Followed by Ministers, Generals, Warriors.

It is as if all mountains, seas, plains and winds,

All who live and yearn in every world

Are massed around them as cloud-banks in the sky.

From a smile,

A jade cup of amrita is offered to you,

And you drink:

4

Light, hovering for an instant within a cloud,

Gives life and play

To moments which the winds bring

And carry off.

Losing yourself and returning

As the countless bubbles in a torrent

Burst in air.

Like a golden fish leaping out of a still lake,

Up into the air,

Light in reflection.

Eternal

Light of Sun.

Shambhala opens,

In the unchanging now of heart-light.

To which you always return.

SAMAYA JA

Universes open and collapse. Worlds live and die. Entering world after world, Gesar lives and dies. Entering and leaving thought after thought, he lives and dies.

As Gesar reaches the summit of the mountain pass that looks down over Ling, when at last after many months of hard travel he sees at last his home, Gesar sings:

*

THE RED GARUDA'S SONG OF CONTINUING

On this great wind of sorrow and longing

We rise up.

On this great wind of love and longing,

The all-seeing Red Garuda spontaneously takes form

And carries us aloft.

SO

In the free radiance of space itself,

In the light of ceaseless love,

Our seeing takes shape.

SO

Winds surveying mind and beyond mind;

Where the gold feather-tips
Of the Red Garuda's outstretched wing
Touch the crystal radiance of space,
The wind of truth expands all at once and in all directions.

Where the Red Garuda's hidden tympanum
Is touched by the cold pure air of emptiness,
The bliss of song enfolds the whole of space.

Where the Red Garuda's golden eye
Meets the fire of a rising sun,
The bright visions of the pure world of Shambhala arise
In the center of the human heart
And on the very face of this earth.

Where the Red Garuda's wild love
Draws near to the heart of all,
The unchanging mind of the Rigden fathers,
Clothed in all the richness of the world,

Emerges instantly from the gold and crystal palace of Kalapa

And appears now, free from time.

This is the love that cannot stop:

It is not conditioned according to its outcome.

It passes through the mirage of life and death.

It passes through world and time and concepts of reality.

It is radiant in whatever outer circumstance.

This is the love that is the heart and heartbeat of all human life.

SO

In the free radiance of space itself,

In the light of ceaseless love,

Amid oceans and seas of galaxies,

The universe takes shape.

*

Now, dancing through worlds as they open, flower, rise and fall, Gesar, King of Ling, Lord of the Four Kinds of Warrior, moves towards us, moves away, dissolves, embraces us. He dances through the shimmering realms of non-existence; he is the guide.

*

COLOPHONS AND NOTES

TILOPA COLOPHON

"The Vidyadhara, Chokyi Gyamtso, the Eleventh Trungpa Tulku, is the true, vivid emanation in this place and time of The Deathless Mahasiddha, Tilopa. Thus as the only lineage father and the life of enlightenment itself, he is an unceasing, boundless, torrential river through the polluted desert of this age.

"Although not an atom can be added to the radiant flow of his limiltess compassion nor a word to his imperial wisdom, this has been written with one-pointed devotion and confidence so that no one will ever be parted from him."

NOTES

Tilo Invocation intro. Adapted from   Gandavyuha Sutra, Cleary Shambhala 1 984 p. 267

(1)adapted from The Life and Teaching of Naropa- Herbert V. Guenther

Oxford University Press, Oxford, UK 1963: PP 94-5

KUKKIRIPA COLOPHON

"In this way, the Druk Sakyong, the XI Trungpa, Chokyi Gyatso,

Who is Kukkuripa in person,

Opens the gateway of the ayatanas to the Kingdom of Shambhala

As a pure realm,

As alive in the human heart,

And as a real place on this earth.

"As shown directly by the Dralas of Lha, Nyen and Lu

Throughout the shimmering range of inner and outer phenomena,

The deathless mahasiddha guru and his unceasing consort

Dance and blaze, appearing in myriad forms:

Now as snow peak, as lichen, now as ptarmigan,

Now as tundra, now as caress, now as insight, as pink columbine

Now as daring, as effort, as peach, as water, now as white cloud billow,

Now as sunlight, as gift, as delight, as soaring vulture, as black crow,

As pressure, as shyness, as thought of child, as traffic, as storm-cloud,

Now as alcohol, as wish, as cedar, as Crystal Torch of Maitri, as love.

"So may this great lord never depart, even for an instant,

From us, his sons and daughters, our children,

And every single being whom we chance to encounter.."

NOTES - Sources

Introduction: Gandavyuha, supra – pp. 56-7

Oral teachings of The Druk Sakyong, the Vidyadhara, The Venerable Chogyam Trungpa Rinpoche, The Dorje Dradul of Mukpo Dong.

Oral teachings of His Holiness, Orgyen Kusum Lingpa.

Jo Nang Taranatha(Templeman tr): The Seven Instruction Lineages, Library of Tibetan Works and Archives 1983, pp 66-7

Abhayadata (Dowman tr.): Masters of Mahamudra, State University of NY Press 1985, pp.199-203

Abhayadatta (Robinson tr.) Buddha's Lions, Dharma Publishing 1979 pp 128-130

PP 5-6: adapted from Jamgon Kongtrul (Kunkhyab Choling tr.) Myriad Worlds, Snow Lion 1995, pp. 116-118

pp 8-11 adapted from:The Larger and Smaller Sukhavativyuha (tr. F.Max Muller) in Buddhist Mahayana Texts, Dover 1969,pp, 2-103

P. 2,10,13,H.H.Dudjom Rinpoche (Dorje&Kapstein tr.) The Nyingmapa School of Tibetan Buddhism, Wisdom Publications 1991 P.x Maitreya;P.y Nagarjuna; P.308(Naropa -Means for Attaining the Real)308,P.125 (Magical Net Tantra)

P.13 Tanpai Nyinche, Mahamudra Teaching (Sherab Dorje Tr.) Snow Lion 1995p.81

P.18-19 adapted from(Kvaerne tr.) An Anthology of Buddhist Songs, Oslo-Bergen-Tromso University 1977

PP 13-17 adapted from (Farrow&Menon Tr.) The Concealed Essence of the Hevajra Tantra, Motilal Banarsidas,DELHI1992

P.16 Saraha (HVGuenther tr. The Royal Song of Saraha, University of Washington Press, 1969

PP19-20 adapted from Tsang Nyon Heruka (Nalanda tr.) The Life of Marpa, Prajna Press 1982 ppxxxvi-vii,24-5,79-80.

MEHKHALA AND KANKHALA COLOPHON

"This is the complete unfolding of the pathway of innate, natural non-dual prajna, space itself. Unmoving and unchanging, she is known as shamatha. Utterly dynamic, moving, multiform, she is known as vipassana. Beyond all notions of duality, she is not apprehended by the paths of names and form.

"In order to fulfill the wishes of the only father guru who is Kanha's living son, and so that all his children never hesitate to continue dancing joyfully in the light of razor's edge."

NOTES- Sources:

Oral teachings of The Druk Sakyong, the Vidyadhara, The Venerable Chogyam Trungpa Rinpoche, The Dorje Dradul of Mukpo Dong.

Jo Nang Taranatha(Templeman tr): The Seven Instruction Lineages, Library of Tibetan Works and Archives 1983

Jo Nang Taranatha (Templemantr.) Life of Krsnacarya/Kanha, Library of Tibetan Works and Archives 1989, pp.62-3

Abhayadata (Dowman tr.): Masters of Mahamudra, State University of NY Press 1,885 pp.317-321

Abhayadatta (Robinson tr.) Buddha's Lions, Dharma Publishing 1979, pp. 211-213

p.3-4 adapted from Dowman op cit p. 317

p.4   adapted from Dowman op cit p. 321

p. 10 from the Ratnavali as cited by Gampopa (HVGuenther tr.) The Jewel Ornament of Liberation, Shambhala Pub. 1971, .209

KING INDRABHUTI COLOPHON

"As has been said, the in two thousand five hundred years after the Death of the Victorious One, the Imperial Yana will return. This has been accomplished by the true Sakyong who never departs from the concerns of this world and never abandons his love of beings, the Dorje Dradul of Mukpo Dong, Chogyam Trungpa, the Eleventh Trungpa Tulku. What is written here is merely a hair floating on the inexhaustible golden ocean of his living word. May it serve to fulfill all the wishes of that great lord instantly."
"MANGALAM"

NOTES - Sources:

Adapted from Jonang Taranatha tr. Templeman The Seven Instruction Lineages: Library of Tibetan Works and Archives, Dharamsala 1983, pp 24-5

The Mirror of Nowness:

COLOPHON

"So that the Kingdom of Shambhala may appear swiftly as a true and constant place of refuge for all beings on this earth, this is written drawing on the light shining in the blood ocean which springs from the heart of the Great Sakyong, the Unexampled Dorje Dradul of Mukpo Dong, the purest and kindest of beings in this dark age.

"So may the truth of Shambhala, shining like an endless river of molten gold, flow in ceaseless torrent from the only father to all his daughters and sons instantly. Through them, may it swell across all the world, sweeping away all sorrow May all find complete liberation in the boundless radiance of nowness.

"With the thought of Orgyen Chophel Jigme Dorje and his family, and all children and all families deep within my heart, it is my one-pointed aspiration that this be so, now in this very time, here in this very place."

"SARVA SHAMBHALA MANGALAM"

NOTES-Sources:

Introductions- adapted from Avatamsaka Sutra, tr. Cleary,vol1, Shambhala Pubs. P242, 243

(1) adapted in part from A Geography and History of Shambhala-Garje K'am-trul Rinpoche pp 3-8 The Tibet Journal Vol3 #3 Autumn 1978)

(2) P.7- Ives Waldo (tr) The Vajra Sunshiner, Mipham Rinpoche's Commentary on the Kalachakra Tantra, unpublished : p.66/100

(3)ibid. p 30/ 38-9

(4)ibid. p.21/28.4

(5)ibid. p.62/ 78

(6)ibid. p.36/48

(7)ibid p.44/60

(8)ibid p.18/25

(9)ibid p.25-6/36

(10)ibid p.250/332

(11)ibid p.253/336

(12)ibid   p.250- 259/332-342

***

GLOSSARY

Abhisheka: (lit. sprinkling or anointing) Ceremony of empowerment enabling the recipient to do certain practices and reach certain kinds of attainment. There are four empowerments relating to body, speech, mind and their essence.

Acarya: (lit. teacher) Title given to certain lineage holders.

Amrita: (lit: anti-death) That which sustains beyond life and death; that which intoxicates conventional views.

Ashe: (lit. primordial stroke) The stroke that cuts through doubt,and aggression towards self and other.

Bhagavan: blessed one

Bhumipala: Earth Protector

Bindu: (lit. dot or point) mind essence

Buddha: (lit. the awakened one)

Co-emergence: simultaneity of wisdom and ignorance

Dakini: (lit. sky-goer) wrathful or semi-wrathful female deity embodying co-emergent wisdom

Dharma: (lit. law or truth) usually here the Buddhist teachings, but may in other contexts refer to normative teachings of other kinds.

Dharmadhatu: (space of phenomena) all encompassing space

Drala: (lit. above enemy) The worldly and transcendent power inherent in direct perception of phenomena. The worldly dralas are the specific communicative nature of sky, mountains, earth, water and the underground.

EVAM: Union of prajna and upaya, wisdom and method, space and phenomena.

Garuda: Mythical Indian Bird that is fully-grown on emerging from the egg, thus a symbol of the awakened mind.

Heruka: (lit. blood drinker) wrathful male embodiment of wisdom flourishing in whatever circumstances he finds himself.

Jnana: Wisdom, spontaneous presence

Kalapa: The capitol city of the Kingdom of Shambhala

Kapala: skull cup

Karma: (lit. action) the continuum of cause and effect, action and result

Kaya: (lit. body) form, as in the three bodies or forms of the Buddha: Dharmakaya (body or form of truth); Sambhogakaya (body or form of enjoyment); and Nirmanakaya (emanation body as manifest in physical form).

Ki and So: The syllables of the warrior cry bring down the power of Drala and Werma

Kroda: wrathful male deity

Lungta: (lit. wind horse) The basic energy of wakefulness.

Mahamudra: (lit. Great Seal). A lineage of meditative traditions in which all experiences are realized in their essential nature as joining prajna and skillful means. Here the vividness of experience is spontaneously realized as the luminous display of the deity.

Mahasiddha: (lit great accomplished one) An accomplished lineage master.

Nadi: The inner pathways of the body through which the bindu moves.

Naga: Serpents, dragons and those treasure holders who dwell beneath the earth or sea.

Padma Sambhava: lit: The Lotus Born. The great Indian teacher, regarded as the second Buddha, who brought Tantric Buddhism to the Himalayas

Phurba: three-bladed dagger which penetrates passion, aggression and ignorance

Prajna: (lit. highest knowledge) the natural precision of awareness that penetrates all dualistic obstacles.

Prana: (lit. wind) inner energy by which the bindu moves through the nadis.

Rigden: The title of the rulers of Shambhala, meaning Holder of the Castes

Rigpa: Ceaseless primordial awareness, the basic awareness that underlies and continues through all mental states, sleeping, wakefulness, life and death

Samadhi: (lit: absorption or concentration) sometimes a synonym for meditation.

Samsara: The endless cycle of painful illusion caused by ignorance, grasping and fixation.

Shambhala: An enlightened society in the human realm.

Shamatha: (lit. Taming or calming the mind) Letting the mind rest in the space in which thoughts arise, dwell and decay.

Siddha: one who has siddhi

Siddhi: An aspect of realization in which the inseparability of relative and absolute reality manifest as power over apparent phenomena..

Sugatagharba: As in Tathagathagharba, innate enlightenment, but here the emphasis is on its experiential component.

Sunyata: (lit. emptiness) The realization that self and other are merely temporary and insubstantial constructs, and that reality itself is completely free from any kind of conceptual or emotional biases.

Tathaghatagharba: (lit. Buddha nature) Intrinsic complete natural wakefulness

Tilopa: The 10th-century Indian Mahasiddha who received the Mahamudra teachings directly from primordial awareness itself and passed them down in the lineages that became today the Kagyupa.

Upaya: (skillful means) The methods by which the inner realization of the lineage is conveyed.

Vajra: (lit. thunderbolt) a ritual object in the form of a five- or nine-pointed thunderbolt that symbolizes the indestructible nature of wisdom and the awakened state.

Vajrayogini: The great dakini who is the essence of co-emergence and the principle of the natural transformation of ignorance and passion into wisdom and skillful means.

Vajrasattva: (lit. Vajra being) The principal of the innate purity if the awakened state.

Vipassana: (insight) That aspect of meditation that relates to mind as motion (as distinct from Shamatha which relates to the unmoving aspect); clear seeing into the patterns of mind and phenomena.

Werma: Lineage of ancestral protectors who may particularly ensure prosperity.

Yidam: A deity through which the practitioner uncovers her or his own awakened nature.

Yogi: male practitioner

Yogini: female practitioner

Made in United States
Orlando, FL
09 February 2024

43487055R00178